THE AMERICAN SANCTUARY MOVEMENT

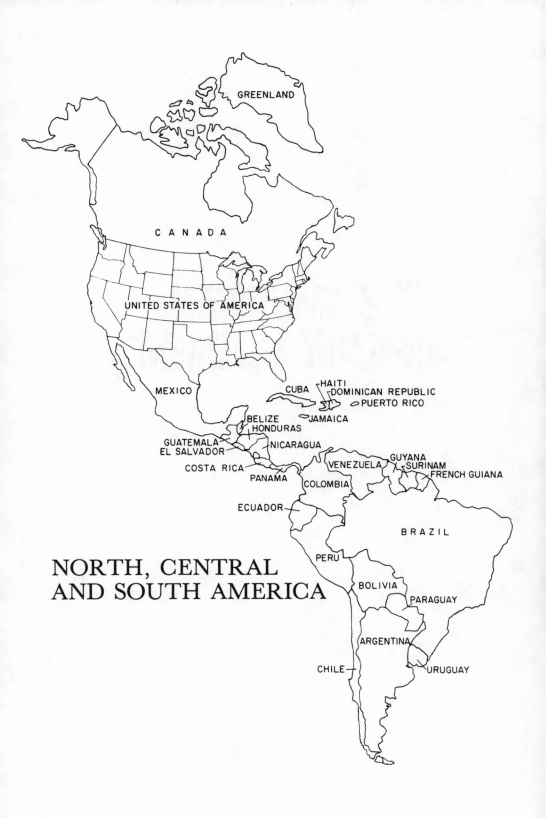

GREENLAND

C A N A D A

UNITED STATES OF AMERICA

MEXICO

CUBA HAITI
DOMINICAN REPUBLIC
PUERTO RICO
JAMAICA

BELIZE
HONDURAS
GUATEMALA
EL SALVADOR NICARAGUA
COSTA RICA
PANAMA
VENEZUELA GUYANA
SURINAM
FRENCH GUIANA
COLOMBIA

ECUADOR

BRAZIL

PERU

NORTH, CENTRAL
AND SOUTH AMERICA

BOLIVIA

PARAGUAY

ARGENTINA

CHILE URUGUAY

THE AMERICAN SANCTUARY MOVEMENT

BY ROBERT TOMSHO

★
TexasMonthlyPress

Texas Monthly Press, Inc.
P.O. Box 1569
Austin, Texas 78767

  B C D E F G H

Library of Congress Cataloging-in-Publication Data

Tomsho, Robert, 1953—
  The American sanctuary movement.

  1. Sanctuary movement.   2. Refugees, Political—Central America.
3. Church work with refugees—United States.   I. Title.
HV645.T65   1987   261.8'32   87-10228
ISBN 0-87719-067-4

Dustjacket design by Ray Sturdivant
Map design by Richard Balsam, Austin Boardworks

To Lesley, my wife, for her love, patience, and encouragement.

SANCTUARY CHURCH SITES
IN THE UNITED STATES

CONTENTS

FOREWORD

In the spring of 1982, I began traveling to the Rio Grande Valley of Texas to report on illegal immigration for a San Antonio newspaper. In the process, I rode with overworked Border Patrol officers, visited detention facilities, and spoke with deportees waiting to be sent home. The focus then was on illegal immigration from Mexico. Every year, thousands upon thousands of that country's citizens cross into our country looking for work or a better way of life.

One afternoon, a Border Patrol officer in Del Rio told me they had been catching an increasing number of OTMs, which I later learned meant "Other Than Mexicans." In the weeks that followed, I sought out some of those people. Most were Salvadorans and Guatemalans. They were not people who joked about being sent home. Some told me they were certain it would mean death.

Those conversations in church basements and detention cells made me want to know more about both the conflict to the south and the government in Washington that was sending the OTMs back to it. This book is a result of that curiosity. It is not meant to be the final word on the sanctuary movement, Central America, or Reagan policies. I will leave that to future historians. I have written this book in hopes that it will inspire readers to listen to the voices of the Central Americans within our borders and consider them in light of our own traditions of democracy and compassion.

There are a great many people to thank for helping me, many

of whom I cannot name. Dozens of Salvadorans and Guatemalans, both in this country and in theirs, told me their stories not knowing whether my use of the information would lead to their deportation or death. I am grateful to them for such trust. In several places in the book, the names of these people have been changed. For their safety, I have also used false names for most of the people I interviewed in Central America.

In addition, I would also like to thank my colleague and friend, John Burnett, a reporter with National Public Radio, who provided me with the benefit of his experience in Guatemala. My thanks also go to the woman identified in this book as "Rebecca," who made certain I did not get into trouble while traveling through Guatemala. *Dallas Morning News* Central America bureau chief Chris Hedges and his wife, Josyane Sechaud, were more than generous with their help, hospitality, and insight during my visit to El Salvador. I am also in debt to the journalist and church worker who acted as my guides there.

Melissa Houtte, my editor at the *Dallas Morning News,* offered nothing but support and encouragement during the time I spent working on this book. Without the initial enthusiasm and continued patience of Scott Lubeck and Anne Norman at Texas Monthly Press, I would never have started or finished the project.

R.T.

INTRODUCTION

"I Am More Afraid to Remain Silent"

On a cool October morning, Juan sits on a legless couch in the basement of an old church in San Francisco's Mission District. A small man of thirty-four years, he has thick black hair, dark eyes, and a sparse moustache. Slumped low in the old couch, he talks about El Salvador, the tiny Central American nation where he was born. Occasionally, he speaks with the wistfulness of a man recalling old times and familiar faces. But mostly, his voice quivers between rage and fear. His parting memories are of jail cells and beatings. That is why he asks to be known only by his first name. He does not want a brother or cousin to get the same treatment because of something he has said here.

Juan has no proof that the authorities back in El Salvador would harm his family. No documents, newspaper clippings, or notarized threats from the chief of police. In fact, he has no evidence of his story, at least none he thinks would convince U.S. immigration authorities that he is worthy of political asylum. Juan can only recall his nightmares and display his scars, as he does this morning.

He hikes up the right leg of his faded jeans and pushes down his sock. The skin heaped across his ankle is a hideous gnarl of red, pink, and purple. It looks as though someone poured candle wax onto his bones and then poked and stirred it until dry. This, says the former medical student, is where the first bullet hit.

Rolling back the left sleeve of his work shirt, he points to a hard knot of tissue. That shot broke his arm. He slowly makes a fist. The little finger won't curl. The nerves never healed.

Juan drops his head and pulls back a shock of hair above his left temple. The bullet that grazed him there left a hairless H-shaped scar.

The bullets were fired one afternoon in December 1980. He and some other medical students had just finished another day working at the Domus María refugee camp near San Salvador. They were standing outside the camp, waiting for a bus back to town. A truckload of National Guardsmen arrived first. The soldiers climbed down and opened fire with their automatic rifles. Juan did not lose consciousness when the three bullets knocked him to the pavement. He didn't lose consciousness until the soldiers tossed him into the back of a truck with the bodies of the dead.

In 1977, Juan and some other medical students from the National University began donating their services to the poor. There were hundreds of thousands of them in El Salvador, one of the most impoverished nations in the Western Hemisphere. The average per capita income each year is still below $900. The students tended to families who lived in the stick and tin shanty towns around the capital, often working within sight of fine mansions with tile roofs, iron gates, and security fences. After the war began in 1979, people from the small towns and villages sought shelter in the refugee camps around the capital. When that happened, Juan and the others took their clinics there.

It was a time when merely teaching the catechism was a subversive activity, a time when the bodies of union organizers and political activists were found daily in body dumps around town, a time when refugees were dragged from their squalid camps by armed men.

In a land where suspicion was grounds for murder, the medical students' act of compassion was viewed as a threat to national security by the right-wing death squads and factions of the security forces.

After the shooting, Juan woke up blindfolded and naked. He was tied to stakes driven into the floor of his cell. The interrogations lasted for twenty-four days. They accused him of treating Communists and guerrillas and demanded to know the names of the doctors, nurses, priests, and nuns with whom he had worked.

The men questioning him said they had found weapons and sub-versive literature in the homes of his friends. Why was he associating with such people? Didn't he love his country? Why didn't he work for the government?

On rare days, his interrogators were friendly. They would make small talk and ask him to write them prescriptions. But most of the time, instead of sharing cigarettes, they put them out on his skin. Other days, they would punctuate their questioning with a fist or boot. During his time as a prisoner, Juan was introduced to a variety of tortures. There was the *capuche,* an airtight canvas or leather mask that made it impossible to breathe. Often, to sharpen the agony, the inside was dusted with lime. Juan was also subjected to the "airplane," wherein they would bind his arms and legs to his body, tie a rope around his waist, and suspend him face down from the ceiling. The guards would then take turns slamming his head into the wall. Sometimes, one of them would ride on his back.

Juan dreaded the electric shocks the most. They would douse his body with ice water, attach alligator clips to his earlobes, tongue, and testicles, and then experiment with various current levels. A few years earlier, Juan had helped administer electrical shocks while serving an internship at a psychiatric unit. He had never realized they made one feel as though his whole body had been slammed by a giant fist, never knew one actually saw stars or woke up exhausted and wanting to cry.

"The truth is, I did not expect to live," he says. "I thought that they would get bored and I would be tossed into the streets as a dead person."

As he waited for death, Juan also thought of the baby he and his girlfriend were expecting. He did not believe he would live to see it, but his conscience was clear. "I thought I was leaving her a good example of who I had been."

Eventually, a relative with friends in the security forces was able to gain Juan's release. By that time, worms had infested his untreated wounds and he had lost all feeling in his left hand. When his uncle carried him out of the National Guard head-quarters, he weighed less than seventy-five pounds.

Juan returned to his village. After local authorities harassed his family, he moved in with a friend. His classmates from the medical school were afraid to come and treat his wounds, so he tried to take care of himself. Eventually, fear, pain, and the fighting going on in the area made him decide to flee.

A friend smuggled Juan to Guatemala City under a truckload of onions, but he ran into problems with the constant security checks by the Guatemalan security forces, who had perfected their own means of torturing suspected subversives. After two months, Juan left Guatemala City for Mexico, following the path tens of thousands of Salvadorans and Guatemalans had traveled before him.

He stayed for a brief time in the refugee camps along the border between Mexico and Guatemala before a church there helped him get to Mexico City. He spent two years there, working in a restaurant. When Mexican police learned he was a Salvadoran, they badgered him constantly, often demanding bribes in exchange for not deporting him. Eventually, he decided to leave Mexico. He hated the harassment and, with his wounds healed, he wanted to speak out about what he had seen in his homeland.

He had hopes of going back to El Salvador, but when he was ready to leave Mexico City, the death squads back home were still littering the streets with corpses. He knew that returning from several years in exile would make him even more suspect than before. Where, they would ask, had he been? Why did he not have papers to prove it? So Juan took a train to Tijuana. There he watched the smugglers leading Mexicans across the border into California. One day, he followed.

An estimated half million Salvadorans and Guatemalans have surged across this country's southern border since 1980. To get here, they have abandoned their homelands and families, sold their possessions, and traveled across hundreds of miles of strange and dangerous terrain. The Reagan administration says they have come because of money—not a desire for democracy or fear of repression. They are simply another wave of Third World poor seeking a piece of the American dream. It is the explanation offered again and again by smartly dressed federal officials who have never even imagined finding their spouse's headless body along a Potomac jogging path or watching a truckload of federal troops gun down commuters at a Georgetown bus stop.

But there has been another reaction from thousands of church people from Seattle to Boston. They have decided to defy their country's immigration policies after encountering a Central American such as Juan. Some have been moved after seeing human bodies that have been ripped by ropes, knives, or bullets. Others have acted after listening to the refugees who have spoken from their pulpits. On March 24, 1982, a handful of churches announced that they would offer the Central American refugees shelter, protection, and a forum from which to speak. Since then, more than 300 other congregations have made similar decisions.

The Reagan administration was tolerant for a time, but once the sanctuary movement became too large, too loud, and too defiant, it dispatched its prosecutors to destroy it.

One corner of the small, dank room where Juan sits is piled high with plastic bags full of old clothes and shoes he has helped collect for other Central American refugees in the Bay Area. Crates of overripe bananas, wilted lettuce, and blackened pears litter the floor. More donations. Every few minutes a mouse scampers between them.

When he is not painting houses or mowing lawns, Juan helps other refugees find food, clothing, and shelter. When he first arrived in San Francisco, Juan was sheltered in a sanctuary church. Today, he continues telling his story to church and school groups, even though each talk puts him in jeopardy. Capture by the Immigration and Naturalization Service could mean deportation to El Salvador.

"I still have plenty of fear," he says. "But I am more afraid to remain silent. My fear here is nothing compared to that of my friends and family back home."

Although the possibility of political asylum exists, Salvadoran applicants routinely have been turned down by the Immigration and Naturalization Service. "Why should I apply when they are denying all the asylum visas?" he asks. "Ninety-seven percent have been denied. Many have worse cases than me."

But asylum or no asylum, for the aspiring doctor this country will never be home. He did not want to come here. In fact, he felt

like he was betraying his country when he did. But by staying and
exposing his scars to strangers, Juan hopes he can make a few
more North Americans understand what is happening just a few
hundred miles south of their border.

"You have beautiful concepts here," he says with a smile. "You
believe in truth. The people react when they hear the truth."

1

A Meeting in the Desert

When Jim Dudley put on his pants on the morning of May 4, 1981, he was not thinking about sending shock waves to Washington or spawning any sort of political movement. Driving the battered gray van down from the mountains above Hermosillo, Mexico that hot day, the thirty-nine-year-old carpenter had other things on his mind.

In a few weeks, he and some other Quakers would be moving to Hermosillo for the summer to run a camp for young Quakers from the United States and Mexico. Every year, the group went to a different village and undertook a project. That summer, they planned to build a chapel for a small community up in the mountains. Dudley had spent the weekend hauling furniture to the site in a van he had borrowed from his friend, Jim Corbett, of Tucson.

Hermosillo is the capital of Sonora, the Mexican state just south of Arizona. A center of agriculture and industry, the city of five hundred thousand is a prosperous place with tree-lined boulevards and tile walks. It is also the last major Mexican city before the Arizona border, 170 miles to the north. That makes Hermosillo a gathering place for smugglers who, for a price, help Mexicans and Central Americans enter the United States illegally.

But this was not Dudley's concern as he drove past mile after mile of tangled desert brush, faded green cactus, and rugged mountains. Dudley planned to drive straight through to Tucson, visit with Jim Corbett and his wife, Pat, for a few hours, and then

catch the 3 A.M. bus back to New Mexico. He had known the
Corbetts for about a year. Jim, also a Quaker, was working on
another project in the Sonoran desert outside Hermosillo. He and
some other Quakers had been helping Mexican ranchers introduce a new breed of goats into their herds.

Dudley pulled into the U.S. border checkpoint at Nogales, Arizona, late that afternoon. It was not much of a border, really. Unlike in Texas, there was no river to divide the two countries. A
chain link fence rambled down from the hills and separated
Nogales, Arizona, from the Mexican city that shared its name.
The people in the two cities regularly crossed the border to shop
and to visit. Even for Mexicans without papers, the fence was
more of a nuisance than a barrier. Countless holes opened onto
the backyards and fields of Nogales, Arizona. Some were even
watched by unofficial "gatekeepers" who charged a toll.

Churches in both cities helped the Mexicans and Central
Americans bound for the United States. On the Mexican side, the
Rev. Ramón Dagoberto Quiñones tended to their needs at his
Catholic church, the Sanctuary of Our Lady of Guadalupe. After
coming through the fence into Arizona, the aliens often headed
for the Sacred Heart Catholic Church. Built on a high hill facing
Mexico, the tall adobe church could be seen from nearly any part
of town. One could always find help there, whether the need was
food, shelter, or maybe a little money. It had always been this
way.

Within a few years, priests and lay workers from both churches
would be arrested for their work with aliens from El Salvador and
Guatemala; Dudley would indirectly be the cause, although he
had no way of knowing it on that warm May afternoon. The carpenter was just going home.

After Dudley answered the customs agent's questions about
citizenship and length of stay, he drove up the hill, past the Wal-
green's, the McDonald's, and the Safeway. After twisting through
the little town, the road ran right into Interstate 19, his route for
the last fifty miles to Tucson.

Almost as soon as he got on the highway, Dudley saw a small,
dark-haired man hitchhiking. He pulled over and offered the
stranger a ride to Tucson. If he was hoping to pass the last few

miles with a little small talk, Dudley had made a mistake. His Spanish was rusty and that was the only language the hitchhiker spoke. Still, as the truck rolled along the two men forced a little conversation through the language barrier, each repeating himself until the other understood.

The hitchhiker was a Salvadoran trying to reach San Francisco. The Border Patrol had already caught and deported him once. The man had been in some sort of trouble in El Salvador, but Dudley did not have time to learn the details.

The two men had only been riding for a few minutes when they approached the Border Patrol's roadblock near Peck Canyon. Traffic cones directed all vehicles to the small trailers parked there. In the few seconds that passed before they stopped, the hitchhiker begged Dudley to tell the Border Patrol that he worked for him and that they were traveling to Tucson together.

Dudley was not sure what to do. He had never been through this before. But when the border patrolman came up to the truck window, Dudley explained that he and his passenger were traveling together. The man in the uniform was not convinced. He told both men to get out of the van. Dudley was led into one of the trailers. Another agent took the Salvadoran somewhere else for questioning.

Dudley quickly admitted he had picked the man up hitchhiking. A few minutes later, the second patrolman returned and told Dudley that they had learned that his passenger was an illegal alien from El Salvador. Beyond that, the patrolman said the man claimed he had paid Dudley $200 to drive him to Tucson. That would make Dudley a smuggler, the officer added. Dudley disputed his hitchhiker's story and after a few more minutes of questioning, the border patrolman told the carpenter he was free to go. The hitchhiker would have to stay behind.

The sun was sinking toward the western edge of the desert by the time Dudley pulled back onto the highway. There were other things on his mind now. He kept thinking of the look on the Salvadoran's face as they approached the roadblock. Why had the man been so afraid? Had he made some telltale blunder to betray his passenger's identity? Could he have taken some other road? What might he have done differently? Dudley was still rolling it through his mind an hour or so later when he stopped the van in front of Jim and Pat Corbett's home in northeast Tucson.

Before ever meeting the Corbetts, a visitor could tell they were different from the people who lived around them. Most of the streets in the neighborhood were lined with roomy ranch-style homes that would fit comfortably into the suburbs of Atlanta, Sacramento, or Pittsburgh. The Corbetts' small brown adobe house looked like it had been plucked up out of the desert and deposited ever so awkwardly in the middle of a subdivision. It sat at one end of a rutted dirt road off one of the main streets. The Corbett compound also included a two-stall stable and a corral out back for Pat's horse. The goats, geese, and chickens had their own pens.

The animals were all that remained of their days ranching along the border. They had sold their spread after arthritis crippled Jim so badly that he could no longer work the land. His hands were as twisted and gnarled as a tangle of old roots. The disease had bent his toes around each other until the only shoes that would fit comfortably were cheap canvas loafers that he bought several sizes too large. The arthritis had weakened his heart as well, although that was not as obvious.

Despite the handicap, Jim Corbett remained a picture of Southwestern grit and determination. Tall and rangy, he favored the faded jeans and pearl-snap shirts worn by desert ranchers. Years under the Arizona sun had wrinkled and reddened his skin and pushed his brow down into a permanent squint. Under his silver-gray hat, he kept a pair of horn-rimmed glasses perched on his long, thin nose. A scraggly patch of beard covered his upper lip and chin. It made him look a bit like a beat poet, but lent his face a wry, ironic look as well.

Corbett, born in Casper, Wyoming, in 1933 was not the sort who was comfortable drifting along in the middle-class mainstream of America. He was a dedicated and sometimes eccentric nonconformist. This was probably not surprising for a man whose family tree included Blackfoot Indians, Kentucky pioneers, and Ozark Mountain mule traders.

Corbett's father, a country lawyer from Missouri, had given up his practice at the onslaught of the Depression and gone to Wyoming to teach school. His mother brought in extra money substitute teaching. The 1930s were tough years for the Corbett family. During the summers they moved across the state to a Shoshone Indian reservation, where they kept food on the table by foraging for berries and fishing for trout.

Corbett was an excellent student. His family hoped to send him to the University of Wyoming, but Jim won a scholarship to Colgate, a feat his parents first heard about in the local paper. At a time when most college students were itching to find a place in the booming postwar economy, Corbett decided to study philosophy. He earned his degree in three years, then went to Harvard on a Woodrow Wilson Fellowship. It took him one year to earn the master's degree that would have made him a welcome addition to any college faculty. Instead, he got married and returned to Wyoming to ranch. His wife never adjusted to ranch life, and after a few years of marriage and three children, they divorced.

By that time, Corbett's parents had moved to a ranch in the Huachuca Mountains near Tombstone, Arizona. To recover from the divorce and the first signs of arthritis, Corbett went there for a few months. After deciding he should try to earn some sort of degree that could help him make a living, he went west to study library science at the University of Southern California.

He met Pat there. Six years his junior, the tall, outdoorsy woman was the daughter of bedrock Southern California conservatives. Her father was a prosperous attorney. Her mother was membership chairwoman for the local Republican party. Pat's passion was horses. As a girl, she spent much of her time grooming and showing them. After she married Jim Corbett in 1962, there was not a great deal of money for such luxuries.

Corbett took a job as philosophy instructor and head librarian at Cochise College in Douglas, Arizona. He and the school administration never saw eye to eye. When college officials tried to censor another instructor's reading list and later the work of a visiting artist, Corbett protested. He also called the actions to the attention of the American Library Association and the American Association of University Professors. At the end of Corbett's first year at Cochise, his contract was not renewed. The arthritis had gotten much worse by then and the Corbetts moved to Los Angeles so Jim could get treatment.

They went back to ranching in the Huachucas in 1966. Jim counseled draft resisters in Tucson during the Vietnam era, but mostly they stayed at the ranch. By 1977, Jim's arthritis was so bad they had to give up the land and move back to Tucson. They lived on Jim's disability checks and the money Pat earned from a part-time job at the University of Arizona. Jim occupied himself with the Sonora goat project and a scholarly study of bees.

After dinner, Jim Dudley, the Corbetts and another visitor talked for hours about Dudley's encounter with the Salvadoran. Although the Corbetts were by no means experts on immigration law, they had ranched along the border long enough to know about the cat-and-mouse game between the Border Patrol and illegal aliens. But the more they talked about it that night, the more they realized that the Salvadorans might be different from the Mexicans. They had seen the headlines about the civil war going on in the tiny Central American country. They had read the year before about the murder of Archbishop Oscar Romero and the four North American churchwomen. The Corbetts' other visitor mentioned that he had heard something about returning Salvadorans who were shot at the San Salvador airport.

Of course, all of them knew about the incident the previous July in the desert near Ajo, about eighty miles west of Tucson. Everybody in southern Arizona knew about it. Some middle-class Salvadorans, loaded down with suitcases full of winter clothes, had tried to enter the United States through the desert. The smugglers they had paid to lead the way got lost and then abandoned them. Reduced to drinking cologne and urine, thirteen of twenty-six had died before the Border Patrol found the survivors. Several Tucson churches had taken them in.

The four friends agreed that it must be a pitiful situation in El Salvador for people to try so hard to leave. Still, there did not seem to be much a person in the United States could do about it. The conversation did not ease Dudley's guilt and concern. As his bus rolled toward Albuquerque that night, he kept thinking about the Salvadoran's frightened face. It was still bothering him the next morning. He called the INS office in Tucson and asked what had happened to the hitchhiker. The person who answered the phone could not offer specifics. The Border Patrol picked up dozens of people every day. Dudley was politely told that usually the Salvadorans were detained for awhile and then flown back to El Salvador.

Dudley hung up the phone thinking that there had to be some way he could help. In Tucson, his friend Jim Corbett had gotten out of bed that morning feeling the same way.

Corbett got the same response when he called the Tucson INS office. He pressed for more information, but they told him that, unless he was an attorney and knew the Salvadoran's name, they couldn't offer any information. Corbett took the brusque response as a challenge. He called the INS office again and asked to speak to someone in charge.

"This is Jim Corbett," he announced, not bothering to mention that he was not the same Jim Corbett who was a judge in Tucson. This time he demanded to know what had happened to the Salvadoran man the Border Patrol had apprehended the day before at Peck Canyon. He got an answer. The man was being held in the Santa Cruz County Jail in Nogales.

Corbett called the Rev. Ricardo Elford. The Tucson priest worked with the Manzo Area Council, a small local group that had been bonding aliens out of detention and providing them with legal counsel. For months, the priest also had been holding weekly prayer vigils outside the Tucson Federal Building. They began as a protest of the shooting of a Chicano boy by a South Tucson policeman, but after Elford and other Tucson clergy began caring for the Ajo survivors, the vigil's focus turned to Central America.

Elford told Corbett no Manzo lawyers were available to go to Nogales. They were trying to gain the release of some Salvadorans who had just been picked up on a nearby Indian reservation. Corbett would have to go himself. Elford advised that, before he could think about getting the Salvadoran released, he would first have to get the man to sign a G-28, an INS form designating legal counsel. By signing the form, an alien could not be deported without a hearing.

With a blank G-28 in hand, Corbett headed for Nogales. At the jail, he found three Salvadoran men, including the one picked up by Dudley the day before. Not wanting to leave before all three Salvadorans had signed the G-28s, Corbett went back to the local Border Patrol office for two more forms. He returned to the county jail about a half hour later only to learn that the Border Patrol had moved the two Salvadorans who had not signed the forms.

Corbett read the Border Patrol's reaction as a challenge. He spent the next week trying to track down the two men before they were deported. In the process, he learned of fifty more Salvadorans who were being held in jails and detention facilities in the area. The overworked Manzo lawyers were finding it nearly impossible to keep up with the growing number of Salvadoran detainees. Those who were bonded out of detention often had no place to go while they completed their applications for political asylum.

Within days after Corbett's trip to Nogales, he and Pat had set aside a few rooms in their home as a small apartment for Salvadorans. He also sent a letter to several dozen Quaker meetings around the country. He wrote about the Salvadoran his friend Dudley had picked up outside Nogales and of the way such people were treated if they were caught by the Border Patrol. He also asked for donations to help pay bonds, then running about $1,000 per alien:

> Of course, ransoming Central American refugees is no more than a beginning. And underlying their problems is a war against the region's dispossessed that is being sponsored and supplied by the U.S. government. But ransoming them is, at least, a beginning.
>
> Speaking only for myself, I can see that if Central American refugees' rights to political asylum are decisively rejected by the U.S. government, or if the U.S. legal system insists on ransom that exceeds our ability to pay, active resistence will be the only alternative to abandoning the refugees to their fate.

Then Corbett appealed to the Friends' sense of history. More than a century earlier, Quakers had operated an underground railroad that helped slaves escape the South. Perhaps in 1981, Corbett suggested, it was time to do it again.

"The creation of a network of actively concerned, mutually supportive people in the U.S. and Mexico may be the best preparation for an adequate response," Corbett wrote. "A network? Quakers will know what I mean."

2

Places of Refuge, Acts of Defiance

Before May was over, Corbett's "network" was propelling him toward a confrontation with the U.S. government. There were only a handful of Arizonans involved then, not enough to merit even passing mention in Tucson papers. But at churches, county jails, and border fences, Corbett and his friends had begun chiseling small holes in U.S. immigration policy.

Ultimately, that meant defying Ronald Reagan, another rugged Westerner who had just been elected president by a landslide. During his campaign, the California Republican had promised to make it more difficult for illegal aliens to enter the United States. A rock-ribbed anti-Communist, Reagan had moved into the White House also pledging to halt Soviet encroachment in the Western Hemisphere. His plan for doing that included giving economic, political, and military support to the same governments the refugees were fleeing.

Corbett was still not all that familiar with Central American politics, but he had heard and believed the refugees' stories about what they had endured at the hands of their governments. A good Quaker just could not turn his back on such people. Beyond that, it irked him that the U.S. government seemed so intent on deporting the Central Americans without hearing them out. Corbett did not mind defying authority if that's what it took to change the situation.

On May 23, 1981, Corbett sent another letter to Quaker friends. This one suggested that they could help Salvadorans avoid capture and deportation from the United States by establishing an information center deep in southern Mexico at Tapachula, the largest city near the Guatemalan border. Tens of thousands of Central Americans were already living in the camps near the frontier. For many, Tapachula was the first stop on their flight to the United States.

In his letter, Corbett proposed that Quakers from Mexico and the United States go to Tapachula to help refugees complete asylum applications. He also advocated starting a newsletter to keep refugees and their supporters informed about routes, travel conditions, and expenses for trips to the United States. Although the letter did not suggest outright that refugee supporters should break U.S. law to help the Central Americans, it clearly placed Corbett against the policy current of the Reagan administration, which was already trying to push a tougher immigration law through Congress and denying most asylum requests from Salvadorans and Guatemalans.

The refugee work began to consume more and more of Corbett's time. In addition to writing letters and calling friends, he was still trying to track down the Salvadorans he had heard of during his first trip to Nogales. On May 30, 1981, Corbett and a Salvadoran acquaintance drove six hours to the INS detention camp at El Centro, California, to see two Salvadorans being represented by the Manzo Council. They also planned to look for a third whom they thought to have been transferred there from the Santa Cruz County Jail in Nogales.

When he learned that one of the Salvadorans had already been deported, Corbett got into an argument with the INS officer in charge. As a result, he left the facility without being able to talk with the other two.

Corbett publicized the incident a week later in a letter sent to friends and reporters. The El Centro confrontation had hardened his resolve to help the refugees and changed his mind about the nature of the problem. "Only a few weeks ago I thought that the systematic violation of Salvadoran refugees' human rights by the Border Patrol and INS was just a symptom of bureaucratic priorities," he wrote. "I now know that I was wrong. The game seems to be the moving of bodies through the deportation channels as fast as possible while maximizing the count, a game in which constitutionally guaranteed human rights are the main obstacles. It's just a matter of efficient administrative plumbing."

Corbett no longer believed the quick deportations of Salvadorans were due to bureaucratic confusion or indifference. To the Tucson Quaker, they were one more manifestation of the United States's desire to maintain the political status quo in Central America. "A flood of refugees from Latin America would, of course, present the U.S. government with numerous political and economic problems, all of them tending to weaken its support of the regimes that produce the refugees," Corbett wrote. "The Border Patrol and the INS have been assigned the job of blocking their escape to the U.S."

Corbett continued going back to El Centro. In June, he was one of several dozen Tucson people who raised nearly $150,000 in cash and collateral to bond Salvadorans out of El Centro. Through his work there and on the border, Corbett's name began to spread among the refugees. In early June, a Salvadoran woman called from Phoenix. She told Corbett some relatives of hers were in Nogales, Mexico. Frightened and uncertain of what to do, they were hiding under a house there. Could he help?

Corbett and two friends drove down late one night, found the Salvadorans, and told them how and where to slip across the border. After they rendezvoused on the Arizona side, he took them to Sacred Heart Church. They were to spend a few days there completing their asylum applications, then Corbett would return, smuggle them past the Border Patrol roadblocks and on to the Tucson INS office to apply for asylum. By making an "affirmative filing" there, Corbett thought the refugees could avoid spending time in a detention camp.

Before he could carry out his plan, Corbett heard about the Rev. Ramón Dagoberto Quiñones, the priest at the Sanctuary of Our Lady of Guadalupe Church in Nogales, Mexico. In addition to sheltering refugees at his church, Corbett learned, the priest said mass every Thursday for inmates of a nearby Mexican prison. Many of the prisoners were Central Americans who had been caught by Mexican authorities. Corbett went across the border and met the Rev. Quiñones.

He soon began spending his Thursdays at the Mexican prison.

While Quiñones said mass for the Mexican prisoners, Corbett, posing as a minister, interviewed Central Americans. He left sheets of paper with them that had his name and address on them as well as advice on how to avoid getting caught when they crossed the border.

Within two months of the day Jim Dudley picked up his hitch-hiker, Corbett was making regular runs to Nogales to smuggle refugees across and take them on to Tucson. With good contacts on both sides of the border and two churches to serve as safe houses, he had also laid the first rails of what would eventually become a modern-day underground railroad stretching from San Salvador and Guatemala City to Seattle, Chicago, and Boston.

By passing out sheets of paper with his name and address on them, he was also making it easy for the INS to discover what he was doing. They soon would.

By midsummer, Corbett had nearly twenty Salvadorans staying at his house. They were strangers to each other, people who had abandoned their homes and in some cases their families to face an uncertain future in the United States. Many had been tortured or watched friends and relatives killed. All had come to Tucson after long and often dangerous journeys. There was little for them to do around the Corbett house. Occasionally, the young men slipped off to drink. Sometimes the tension erupted into arguments and fights.

With her husband spending more and more time driving to and from the border, Pat Corbett was often left to manage on her own. She broke up fights, listened to horror stories, and wielded a mop when the septic tank backed up. The calls for help kept coming, and finally the couple decided that they could not continue the work alone.

Corbett went to several Tucson churches to ask them to house some of the refugees he was bringing back from the border, but he did not have any success until he stopped by the Rev. John Fife's house beside Southside Presbyterian Church.

Fife, a lanky chain-smoker with a deep voice and a face reminiscent of a clean-shaven Abe Lincoln, had met Corbett at the

Thursday afternoon vigils. Fife had also been part of the effort to bond refugees out of El Centro.

Corbett asked the minister if his congregation could house some of the Central Americans he was running up from the border. The congregation was already caring for some of the refugees who had been bonded out of El Centro. But there was a difference. The refugees from El Centro had papers permitting them legally to remain in the United States until their cases were decided. In essence, Corbett wanted the church to harbor illegal aliens.

The preacher had known of and respected the Quaker's one-man smuggling operation for some time, but admiration was a long way from becoming an accomplice in a federal crime. Beyond that, it was not just a personal decision Corbett was asking him to make. Keeping illegal aliens at Southside Presbyterian would involve the 140 members of the church as well. Fife could not make the decision alone, but he promised Corbett that he would bring it up with the congregation's Council of Elders.

Fife had a history of social activism dating back to his seminary days in Pittsburgh. There, in the early 1960s, the Pennsylvanian had been arrested for trespassing and disturbing the peace after he and others picketed some local slumlords. He was jailed again in Selma, Alabama, when he joined Martin Luther King, Jr.'s, voter registration drive there in 1965. From Pittsburgh, Fife went one hundred miles west to Canton, Ohio, where he carried on an urban ministry among the poor in that small industrial city.

By the time he became pastor of Southside in 1970, Fife was chairing a national committee reviewing the Presbyterian church's investments. Using the church's multimillion-dollar stock portfolio as a lever, the committee worked against the manufacture and export of DDT. Its members also tried to convince Ford and General Motors to end their investment in South Africa. Through the committee, Fife also had his first contact with Central America when, in 1977, the committee investigated the murders of several union organizers at a Guatemala City Coca-Cola plant.

Fife brought the same sense of social activism to Southside Presbyterian. Built on a parched strip of land in a barrio just east of Interstate 10, the tiny blue-and-white stucco church lacked the marble columns and stained glass windows that adorned some of its suburban counterparts. Inside, the view was similarly stark. Instead of polished wooden pews, church members sat on metal folding chairs during their Sunday services. And when the minister was not walking among them, he stood in front of a huge wooden cross made of old railroad ties. The church had its poor, but the congregation also included doctors, lawyers, professors, and city cops. There were blacks, whites, and Hispanics, as well as members of four Indian tribes.

Long before their church became the cradle of the sanctuary movement, the members of Southside accepted their pastor's activist stance. He had a policy, for instance, of never turning away someone who was broke, hungry, or homeless. Being so close to the interstate, many such people came to the church. The congregation was also supportive when Fife led the church's youth group in a protest at a local restaurant owned by a company that was then the target of a boycott because of its sale of substandard infant formula in the Third World.

Fife lent his name to nearly every social cause that seemed to arise, so no one at Southside was surprised when their pastor told the Tucson Ecumenical Council that his congregation would be happy to provide social services to the survivors of the Ajo incident.

The disaster had begun to unfold on the night of July 4, 1980, while the rest of southern Arizona was enjoying the beginning of a long Independence Day weekend. While on patrol near the Organ Pipe Cactus National Monument, about two hours west of Tucson, a Border Patrolman came upon three Salvadorans. All were suffering from severe dehydration. He questioned them, but they denied being part of any larger group.

The following day, a second agent patrolling a highway in the same area was flagged down by another Salvadoran. She told him of friends dying in the desert then led him to the spot. There he found thirteen bodies on the desert floor. The one-hundred-fifteen-degree heat had played grotesque tricks with the rotting corpses. Some had dirt and sand in their mouths and looked as though they had been clawing for water. The eleven survivors still at the scene were not in much better shape.

They had been part of a group of forty-three Salvadorans who had paid smugglers $1,200 each to get them from their country into the United States. The trip had gone without incident until they reached the Mexican city of San Luis Río Colorado, across the border from Yuma, Arizona. When they began their trip, the Salvadorans were promised that a plane would meet them at the U.S.–Mexico border and fly them to Los Angeles. At San Luis Río Colorado, they were told they would have to go across on foot.

Fifteen of the travelers decided to stay behind and make their way across as best they could. Loaded down with plastic jugs of water and suitcases filled with books, toiletries, and winter clothes, twenty-eight others chose to follow the four "coyotes" who were supposed to lead them into the United States. But the smugglers were no more adept at desert travel than their charges. By noon on Friday, July 4, they were lost somewhere in the Arizona desert. Two of the Salvadorans and one of the smugglers took the remaining water and set out to find their way. The trio was caught by the Border Patrol that night. By the time they found the rest of the group, the survivors—who included two of the smugglers—had been reduced to drinking cologne, deodorant, and their own urine.

Reporters from around the country came to Ajo to cover the story. The Border Patrol took the Salvadorans, who were both illegal aliens and witnesses in a murder investigation, into custody. Tucson churches quickly mobilized to help them. The Catholic Diocese and St. Mark's Presbyterian Church put up bond money to get the survivors out of detention. Fife's church provided translators and attempted to find places for the Salvadorans to stay.

Although the Southside congregation was accustomed to helping North Americans who came to the church looking for help, it was the first experience most members of the church had had with Central Americans. Fife began reading up on the troubled region. Having marched with King in Selma, he sympathized with a people's desire to have some say in the course of their lives. Fife's work in this country's civil rights movement also gave him some understanding of the way an entrenched government could brutalize people pursuing such a goal.

Still, nothing in his experience prepared him for the way Salvadoran churchpeople seemed to be singled out for persecution. Fife had not yet visited El Salvador, but being a minister, just reading about the torture and murder of clergy and church workers in El Salvador had a profound impact on him. He began talking about it with his friend, the Rev. Ricardo Elford, a priest who had come to Tucson about the same time as Fife. In hopes of raising public awareness of the issue, they initiated the Thursday afternoon vigils in early 1981.

The vigils quickly became a focal point for Tucson students, professors, social workers, and members of the clergy interested in Central America. As the rush hour traffic began to back up in front of the Federal Building, they would gather with their signs to pray, sing, and trade news about El Salvador and Guatemala. They made contacts that, a year later, would be useful in the sanctuary movement.

Immigration lawyers from the Manzo Council frequently came. After the 1979 revolution in El Salvador, they began seeing increasing numbers of Central Americans at the INS detention centers and local jails. By 1981, Salvadorans and Guatemalans made up a substantial portion of their caseload. At the vigils, Manzo lawyers would report on various Salvadorans in detention and ask churches to raise bond money and to take in refugees while they completed their applications for political asylum.

By April, everyone involved knew the numbers were growing too large for this ad hoc approach. Members of the Manzo Council and the Tucson Ecumenical Council, which had since formed a task force to deal with the refugee work, decided to launch a campaign to raise bond money for the Salvadorans at El Centro. By June, they had raised $30,000 in cash and $110,000 in collateral. A team of about 30 volunteers drove to El Centro and stayed for two weeks, often working through the night to help Salvadorans complete the necessary paperwork. In the end, about 140 were released. The Tucson group had chartered buses for those who wanted to go to Los Angeles, which had more than 200,000 undocumented Central Americans living in its barrios. Those without contacts in California were shuttled to Tucson, where the churches found places for them to stay and provided them with food and social services while their cases moved through the immigration system.

With that as a background, the Southside Presbyterian elders spent more than four hours discussing Corbett's request and finally agreed that they would accept any refugee that Corbett or anyone else brought to the church. They would not ask for papers. When the decision was announced to the congregation the following Sunday, Fife warned that the federal government could charge him and other members with harboring undocumented aliens. No one protested and refugees soon began arriving.

On any given night, there might be from two to twenty-five of them sleeping in the church. The congregation set up a one-room apartment for them behind the chapel. When that was full, the refugees slept on foam pads in the Sunday school wing.

Fife made a point of introducing new refugees during the services and telling their reasons for leaving. Southside families began taking refugees home for dinner and even to live. The church's women's group brought in food several times a month. As the contact grew more frequent, the refugees became more than another issue to which the pastor had lent his name. For the people of Southside Presbyterian, the war in Central America had very literally come home. Some church members even began helping Corbett with his border runs.

That fall, Fife made his first trip to Nogales to pick up refugees. He drove his pickup truck back on the main road, praying luck and the Lord would be with him. After a time, the minister began traveling to Hermosillo to help Salvadorans skirt Mexican checkpoints along the road to the border. He worried about what arrest would mean to his wife and children, but his luck held. "It was just a wing and a prayer operation," Fife recalls. "I think everybody who started it assumed that they were going to get picked up if they kept at it long enough."

One day around Thanksgiving, a federal attorney stopped one of the Manzo paralegals after an immigration hearing. He told her that, although the government was not sure what her friends Corbett and Fife had been up to along the border, investigators were fairly certain the Tucsonians were involved with some sort of smuggling operation. Then he warned her that, if it did not stop, there would be arrests.

Corbett and Fife already knew that a number of Central Americans had been caught while carrying slips of paper with their names and addresses on them. They had assumed from the start that eventually the INS would have to react, but the prosecutor's veiled threat gave them cause immediately to reconsider their method of operation.

A few nights later, members of the Manzo Council and the Tucson Ecumenical Council sat down in Fife's living room to decide what to do next. All agreed they could not stop their work with the refugees, even though continuing would probably mean arrest. Then they began to talk about publicizing their work and the reasons for it. At least that way, if the INS arrested them, they would not appear to be just another bunch of coyotes. Beyond that, it might also serve to heighten public awareness of Central America.

During the discussion, Fife remembered the religious concept of sanctuary. In the Bible, sanctuary had its roots in the book of Numbers, where Moses was commanded to establish "cities of refuge" for "the people of Israel, and for the stranger and for the sojourner among them, that any one who kills any person without intent may flee there." In the centuries that followed, there were other instances of churches being declared safe havens for people fleeing persecution or punishment. In A.D. 324, Emperor Constantine guaranteed sanctuary in Christian churches throughout the Holy Roman Empire. Seven centuries later, William the Conqueror of England declared Westminster Cathedral a sanctuary.

The concept of sanctuary is not recognized in U.S. law, but the discussion group that night decided that using the word would at least give the public some religious and historical justification for what they were doing. They also agreed that, because of its past work with refugees, Southside Presbyterian was best prepared to handle it.

As he had done before, Fife promised to bring the issue before the nine-member church council at its next meeting. The council discussed the issue, studied the Bible, and called in professors from the University of Arizona law school to outline the legal consequences. They were substantial. Anyone convicted of bringing illegal aliens in the United States faced a five-year sentence and more than $2,000 in fines for each alien involved. There were similar penalties for transporting and harboring aliens, or even encouraging them to enter the United States illegally.

In January, the council recommended that the congregation approve the action. After services one Sunday, church members spent more than four hours discussing the issue before taking a secret ballot. Of the sixty-five voting, fifty-nine favored declaring sanctuary, two voted against it, and four abstained. The congregation decided to make its public declaration on March 24, the second anniversary of the assassination of Salvadoran Archbishop Oscar Romero.

The members of Southside Presbyterian did not know it, but in the San Francisco Bay area of California, another group of church people was gradually moving toward the same decision.

The Salvadorans were, by far, the largest group of the Central American refugees. After they filtered across the border, many disappeared into the Hispanic barrios of nearby cities such as San Antonio, Tucson, San Diego, and Los Angeles. But thousands of others extended their journey and made their way to another city, one that had attracted their parents' generation in the years following World War II. By the late 1970s, an estimated sixty thousand Salvadorans lived in San Francisco. In the city's Mission District, there were restaurants, groceries, and small businesses with Salvadoran names. At some churches, most of the congregation was Salvadoran. In San Francisco, a Salvadoran refugee might be able to get help from an old family friend or a distant relative.

The Bay Area was also a place where, long before the crisis in Central America, churches and even cities had defied the federal government with declarations of sanctuary. In 1971, the University Lutheran Chapel, a tiny Berkeley church on the edge of the University of California campus, had offered haven to sailors from the aircraft carrier *Coral Sea,* then bound for Vietnam.

The Rev. Gus Schultz, a soft-spoken Alabaman, had become pastor of the church two years earlier. As a theology student, Schultz had written his graduate dissertation on the work of Dr. Martin Luther King, Jr. He had decided to come to University Lutheran because of its long involvement in the civil rights movement. When Schultz arrived in Berkeley in 1969, the church was deeply involved in the antiwar movement. Every week there were marches and demonstrations on the nearby campus.

The idea of opening the church to military deserters came from Bob Fitch, a local photographer and minister. Fitch knew some sailors about to ship out for Vietnam aboard the *Coral Sea,* then anchored near San Francisco. By offering the deserters sanctuary in the church, Fitch argued, University Lutheran could make a powerful antiwar statement. Schultz offered the idea to the members of his church, many of whom had been active in antiwar marches and rallies. They embraced it and a few weeks later, with five sailors waiting in the basement of the church, Schultz and a few other ministers held a press conference.

On November 10, 1971, the Berkeley City Council declared the city a sanctuary and ordered city employees not to aid the federal government in investigating the sanctuary churches. Before the war wound down, twenty-two Bay Area churches had either declared sanctuary or offered support to congregations that had. Hundreds of servicemen came to the churches seeking help with a variety of problems ranging from drug addiction to being absent without leave. Sixteen servicemen sought refuge in the churches. Eventually, all were either arrested or, with the help of the church sanctuary committee, able to negotiate discharges. Never, during the entire controversy, did military police enter a church sanctuary to make an arrest.

During the fall of 1981, Schultz and some other Berkeley ministers who met every Tuesday for lunch and Bible study began discussing Central America during their weekly sessions. When one of the ministers mentioned the huge number of Salvadorans being deported, Schultz suggested that they consider reviving the sanctuary concept. But since few refugees had settled in the campus area, the group asked Eileen Purcell of Catholic Social Services in San Francisco to come talk to them.

Purcell, an intense, dark-haired woman, had a job with Catholic Social Services in San Francisco. With the Rev. Cuclam Moriarity, an elderly Irish priest at a small San Jose parish, she began looking into the reasons why the new wave of Salvadorans was coming to San Francisco. They also hoped to determine how the church could best respond. During the summer of 1980, she spent nearly a month touring El Salvador at the invitation of the archdiocese there. "It was my transforming experience," she says. "They had just closed the [National] University. We could see machine gun holes in virtually every building at the university. There were bodies in the streets. There were decapitated people in front of the theater in downtown San Salvador."

She returned more determined to help the Salvadorans in the United States. The church was behind her. In March 1980, Archbishop John Quinn of San Francisco had gone to El Salvador to attend the funeral of Archbishop Oscar Romero, who had been murdered while saying mass. During the service, Salvadoran security forces opened fire on mourners who had crowded into the plaza outside the cathedral. Quinn returned to San Francisco and renounced the violence at an airport news conference. Nine months later, four Catholic churchwomen from the United States were murdered on a road near the San Salvador airport.

"The impact of both these events was a sanctioning by our hierarchy to enter this work full force," says Purcell, "in terms of social and legal services, but also in terms of the church having a responsibility to raise its voice and criticize social injustice wherever it occurs." Refugees were taken into church rectories and offered medical help at Catholic hospitals. Purcell and others began giving speeches and workshops on refugee issues at parishes throughout the Bay area. In the fall of 1981, she gave one to Gus Schultz's lunch group.

In November 1981, one of the Berkeley churches, St. John's Presbyterian, took in a young Salvadoran couple and their baby son, although there was no public announcement. The couple was not interested in drawing attention to themselves.

A few weeks later, after discussing the matter over a potluck lunch one Sunday, Schultz's congregation voted to revive the sanctuary program it had undertaken ten years earlier. After receiving a letter from Tucson about Southside Presbyterian's plans to declare sanctuary on March 24, University Lutheran targeted the same date for its announcement. In addition to providing shelter and legal assistance, the congregation hoped to attract the attention of San Francisco news media and publicize the issue with area members of Congress. There was only one problem: Schultz could not find a Salvadoran who was willing to take part.

On the Friday before the announcement was to be made, Schultz drove to San Francisco and talked with a Salvadoran he had met through Purcell. Ten years earlier, government agents had been reluctant to enter the church to arrest Navy deserters. Schultz could not guarantee the same reluctance with the refugees, but the church would do all it could to prevent their arrest and deportation. Beyond that, the sanctuary declaration was a golden opportunity to draw attention to the situation in El Salvador. Only the Salvadorans could decide whether it was worth the risk.

On the morning of March 24, three Salvadoran men came to University Lutheran Chapel for the press conference. They included a teenager, a medical student, and a survivor of the disaster in the desert near Ajo, Arizona. They would live at the church for a short time and then move into an apartment provided by University Lutheran and the five other Berkeley churches that had decided to support the sanctuary declaration. No one there that morning was certain where it would all lead.

"It suddenly occurred to us," Schultz recalls, "that we might make a big thing out of the people in these churches and they might ignore it — the press, the government and everybody else."

But reporters were there and, as the founders of the movement would later learn, the government was very definitely paying attention that day. Especially in Tucson.

Signs were posted in the yard beside Southside Presbyterian

Church on the day of its declaration of sanctuary. "This is a sanctuary of God for the oppressed from Central America," one said in Spanish. "La Migra [INS], don't profane the sanctuary," read the command on the other. The press conference began at 10 A.M. Television camera crews and reporters crowded around a long table on the church steps.

Corbett was there to tell them he had been smuggling Central Americans across the border for months. Lawyers from the Manzo Council had come to talk about immigration law. With bandanas wrapped around their faces, the Salvadorans preparing to go into sanctuary were there to speak of their reasons for coming to the United States.

When the press conference began, John Fife pointed to a man standing beside a car parked across the street. The man was an INS agent, he told the crowd. "We're glad to know of their interest," the minister added. "We hope he will accurately report exactly what our position is."

With that, he read a letter the congregation had sent to Attorney General William French Smith:

> We are writing to inform you that the Southside Presbyterian church will publicly violate the Immigration and Nationality Act Section 274(a). We have declared our church as a "sanctuary" for undocumented refugees from Central America. . . . We believe that justice and mercy require that people of conscience actively assert our God-given right to aid anyone fleeing from persecution and murder. The current administration of U.S. law prohibits us from sheltering these refugees from Central America. Therefore we believe the administration of the law to be immoral as well as illegal.

That evening, Fife and several other members of the Tucson clergy led about 250 people in a procession from the Federal Building to Southside Church, where a formal service was planned to welcome the Salvadorans into sanctuary. Agent Thomas Martin of the Tucson Border Patrol office was among the crowd. He later wrote a letter to his superiors describing what happened:

The March began at the Federal Building at
6:30 P.M. Various groups congregated there at that
time. One was the "Young Socialists Alliance" which
had a table set up and was selling books which were of
that ideology. Various priests, ministers, etc., showed
up in their various garb. There were some nuns and
quite a few older people (appearing to be families of the
clergy). There was also a group of older "Latin" appearing people, mostly men, who played guitars and
sang hymns of some kind. . . .

As far as I could tell, there were no El Salvadorans
there. Somebody showed up with about ten placards
about El Salvador, U.S. policy, etc. Eventually, the
march was started . . . led by about ten men who vol-
unteered to carry a hollow 5′ × 10′ cross to the church.
Small candles were handed out to everyone and were
lit, but kept going out. I would estimate there were not
more than 300 people there. Aside from the old people,
most of them looked like the anti–Vietnam war protestors of the early 70s. In other words, political misfits.

Nothing derogatory toward the Border Patrol or
tending to incite anyone to violate any law was
said . . .

I attended the "service" to see what they were going to do. I got a seat near the rear and was given
an "order-of-service" or bulletin. Various TV and
news cameras were set up in the back of the church,
not to mention still photographers. I believe I was
photographed.

The "service" appeared to be purely a political show
with all the ministers, priests, etc. at the altar
area. . . . Various times during the first part of the
"service" while cameras were going, the "Frito Bandito"
appeared in the front doorway . . . I refer to an alleged
El Salvadoran wearing a black mask, who has been
used in various photos.

There was nothing really inflammatory or inciting
said, it was rather bland. It seemed like this "service"

was a political event meant to reassure those still not firmly committed to the overt violation of Federal law [that] everything was alright [sic] and "God is on our side."

It seems that this movement is more political than religious but that a ploy is going to be Border Patrol "baiting" by that group in order to demonstrate to the public that the U.S. Government via its jack-booted gestapo Border Patrol agents thinks nothing of breaking down the doors of their churches to drag Jesus Christ out to be tortured and murdered. I believe that all political implications should be considered before any further action is taken toward this group.

3

El Salvador:
One Family's Flight

The North Americans in Tucson and San Francisco could write defiant letters to Washington knowing that even if their government decided to move against them, the worst they faced was a fine and a few years in prison. Sanctuary workers did not have to fear that punishment would suddenly be meted out at a Border Patrol roadblock or a state police outpost. And none had to worry that, because of their views, they might simply disappear.

The people of El Salvador did not enjoy such guarantees. For them, the violence was always waiting. It had been that way since the leftist guerrillas and the U.S.-backed government began their bloodletting in 1979. By the time the churches in Arizona and California were considering sanctuary, twenty thousand Salvadoran civilians had been killed. The guerrillas were responsible for some of the deaths, but most were committed by the security forces or the right-wing death squads that roamed the country in their black-windowed Jeep Cherokees.

In the impoverished nation of five million, not every family had been touched by the terror, but all knew of its dark and random ways. Neighbors missing. Villages leveled. Roadsides littered with rotting bodies. There was no forgetting. Even when the violence could not be seen it was at the heart of a million little stories passed from friend to friend.

In Washington, D.C., the Reagan administration received reports on the carnage in a weekly "grimgram" from the U.S. Embassy in San Salvador. In the cable for the week of March 20–26, 1982 — the same week the first North American churches were declaring sanctuary—U.S. Ambassador Deane Hinton informed Washington that the Salvadoran press had reported the deaths of ninety-eight persons: "Twelve of the victims were allegedly killed by leftist terrorists. Press reports also revealed the arrest of eight patrulleros (armed auxiliaries of the security forces) and four civilians for the murders of 24 persons early in March . . . The killers of the remaining 62 persons could not be identified. In addition to those killed, a total of eight persons were reported disappeared during the week. The authors of these disappearances could not be identified."

Drawn from news accounts, the U.S. Embassy's tally was usually the most conservative. Many of the murders and disappearances occurred in the countryside, far from the eyes of the Salvadoran press. Those incidents were often reported to the Catholic church's Human Rights Office or one of the private groups. Their figures were always higher. Having experienced the murders of their own leaders, perhaps they were more willing to believe.

A Salvadoran did not have to sign a protest letter or deliver an angry speech to meet such an end. One could be the mother of a young man who had gone off to fight with the guerrillas, the mayor of a village the rebels sought to control, or a worker demanding a living wage. As one young Salvadoran woman, Vicky Martínez, learned, the crime of subversion could also mean instructing Catholic children in the catechism or teaching old peasants to read.

On a sweltering July night in 1985, Vicky Martínez sits on a wicker chair in the sunroom of my Dallas home. She sips iced tea while keeping an eye on her year-old son, Adrián, a plump little fellow with fat cheeks and black hair that has been carefully parted on one side. When the boy pushes his plastic truck into one of the tables, his scolding mother puts him on her lap.

Vicky, twenty-five, is a small woman with long black hair, dark eyes, and a shy smile. In her red summer dress and sandals, she could be a young mother anywhere in the Southwest. But Vicky is uncomfortable here. The North Americans have been friendly during her two years in the United States, but their customs are strange and she still struggles with the language. There is peace in her new country, and the opportunity for a prosperous life. Still, she dreams of returning to El Salvador. It will always be home.

Her husband, Rodrigo García, sits nearby. The Guatemalan army deserter met his wife while they were both refugees in southern Mexico. At twenty-seven, Rodrigo is a stocky man with thick black hair and a wispy moustache. Because he speaks good English, his adjustment to life in the United States has not been so difficult. To support his family, he mows lawns, refinishes furniture, and sometimes works for a social service agency in nearby Fort Worth. Rodrigo earns more money than he would have ever dreamed of in Guatemala, but like his wife, he thinks of going home.

"Last year, we became very unhappy," he says. "We considered moving back to Mexico. We even made some plans, but decided we could do more here.

"Our sense is we do not do this for ourselves," he says of their year and a half of speaking to North Americans about the situation in Central America. "We remember the people killed."

I met Vicky and Rodrigo in the fall of 1984, just a few months after they had been given sanctuary at St. Francis Presbyterian Church, a tiny Fort Worth congregation with no building of its own. We got together at the home of one of the congregation members. Vicky cradled her newborn baby that evening as Rodrigo told me their story. It was one of his first interviews with a North American reporter. He sat on the edge of his chair that night, speaking in torrents of broken English. His voice was almost desperate, as though he feared the night might end before he was able to put their memories into words.

It did. And although we met several more times over the next few months, it was usually so that they could introduce me to other refugees. Since we first met, they have told their story dozens of times to church groups across Texas. Although the passion is still there in Rodrigo's voice, it is laced with fatigue.

"Commonly, we talk to thirty or fifty people," Rodrigo says. "Almost every time, we feel like we are living again what we are telling. For us it is telling the life.

"We think there is going to be great impact," he adds, "but then people are really quiet."

Vicky's father, Lucas Martínez, is also in Texas. A small Catholic parish in South Dallas has given him and his family sanctuary. In El Salvador, Lucas was an administrator at a huge coffee plantation. It was a position that commanded respect. Now, at eighty-five, he finds himself a poor man, an illegal alien, a refugee dependent on the good will of strangers. For a time, Lucas also told his story to reporters and church groups but now he too has tired of it.

"It is very different to talk to the people here," says his daughter. "We feel no one seems to believe us."

Wedged between Guatemala and Honduras, El Salvador is a small country roughly the size of New Jersey. From east to west, it measures about 150 miles, from north to south, about 60. Sandy beaches line the tiny country's Pacific shore. The fertile coastal plain gives way to the chain of volcanoes that run west-to-east from the Guatemalan border all the way to the Gulf of Fonseca, which separates the country from Nicaragua. The volcanoes, some still shrouded in a steamy mist, have blessed El Salvador with rich soil. It is both the country's most important resource and the root of its current problems.

With a population density of about six hundred persons per square mile, El Salvador is the most crowded country on the American mainland. Its five million inhabitants are among the poorest. In 1984, the average per capita income was about $850 per year, although most families lived on far less. Five percent of the nation's families enjoyed 38 percent of El Salvador's income. At the other end of the scale, 40 percent of all families earned only 7.5 percent.

The figures for land ownership are equally skewed. According to a 1975 United Nations report, 40 percent of the population had no access to land while 1 percent owned 70 percent of it.

Such inequities have existed since Pedro de Alvarado and his Spanish troops marched in from Mexico in the 1520s. Although they faced determined opposition from the Pipiles and other Indian tribes living on the land, the Spanish were able to gain control of most of present-day El Salvador by 1540.

During the early colonial years, the Spanish conquerors branded Indian slaves and used them as pack mules and mine workers. After the crown did away with slavery, it instituted the *encomienda* system, in which a Spaniard was given the right to extract tribute from Indians in a region in exchange for teaching them the ways of Christianity.

European diseases, poor living conditions, and forced labor took their toll on the indigenous population, reducing it from an estimated five-hundred thousand when the Spaniards took control, to about seventy-seven thousand less than fifty years later. But with the help of a few slaves imported from Africa, the colonists usually managed to round up sufficient labor to harvest their cash crops.

El Salvador did not have the gold and silver deposits that attracted Spaniards to other New World colonies, but it had been blessed with fertile soil. During the early years, the Spaniards made their fortunes with cacao, which they found the Indians growing when they arrived. Even after the conquest, the plantations were worked and overseen by Indians. The natives were, however, required to market their goods through Spanish and mestizo merchants. The newcomers also demanded tribute payments so stiff that smaller farmers were eventually forced out of business. Their property then went either to the crown or to larger landowners. This, coupled with the death of Indian workers from disease, all but killed the cacao business by 1610.

The Spaniards then turned to indigo. As they were developing this new crop, many established self-sufficient haciendas where they grew corn and other food crops and raised cattle. Through corruption and force, these landowners added what had been Indian land to their holdings. By the time the Federation of Central America gained independence from Spain in 1821, there were still substantial numbers of Indians or mestizo communal farms — known as *ejidos* — in the central and western parts of the country, but the Spanish-owned haciendas covered about one-fourth of El Salvador's land.

By the 1860s, it had become almost impossible to maintain a decent fortune by producing indigo. U.S. demand had declined as a result of its Civil War. The Europeans had turned to synthetic dyes, and those importers who still wanted indigo could find it cheaper in Asia. But the large landowners were quickly learning that El Salvador was perfectly suited for another crop of which the North Americans and the Europeans couldn't seem to get enough.

Coffee rapidly became to El Salvador what cotton had been to the American South in the years before the Civil War. *El grano de oro,* they called it, the grain of gold. The volcanic soil and high elevation of central and western El Salvador were the best places to grow it. Unfortunately for the large landowners, much of that territory was covered with *ejidos.* With their friends in the government, however, this turned out to be only a minor obstacle.

In 1856, the government announed that any *ejido* that did not plant coffee on two-thirds of its acreage would lose its land to the government. Although this delighted plantation owners, bankers, and anyone else with access to credit, it presented a few problems for the *ejido* farmers. The coffee plants had to grow three seasons before they produced a crop. Most peasants had trouble enough feeding their family from year to year. Beyond that, planting coffee would mean less land for the corn and beans that filled the peasants' cook pots. Still, in order to keep their land, some tried to make the transition.

But that was not really what the government had in mind. In 1881, it decreed that all communal land that was not divided up among its owners would revert to the government. A year later, the *ejidos* were abolished altogether. In many areas, the peasants were forcibly evicted from their lands. Between 1872 and 1898, there were five uprisings in the coffee-growing areas, but all were quickly crushed by the plantation owners' private armies, which were later incorporated into the official security forces.

For the peasants, the upheaval translated into higher rates of alcoholism and illegitimate birth along with a general unraveling of their society, culture, and pride. New laws prohibited rural labor unions and forced "vagrants" to work in the coffee fields. With little open land remaining in the crowded country, many *ejido* farmers became day laborers who wandered El Salvador looking for a crop to harvest. The luckier ones moved onto the coffee plantations. In return for subsistence wages and a small plot of land, the *colonos* were granted the privilege of filling the coffee cups of Europe and North America.

By the turn of the century, the best land was owned by fourteen families, or "*la catorce*," as they became known. With the coffee profits, the oligarchy tightened its grip on El Salvador's banks, businesses, and industries. Coincidentally, coffee growers and their military supporters developed an uncanny ability to control the Presidential Palace.

The gap between rich and poor was wide, as Major A. R. Harris, a U.S. military attaché, found when he visited the country in December 1931:

> About the first thing one observes when he goes to San Salvador is the number of expensive automobiles on the streets. There seems to be nothing but Packards and Pierce Arrows about. There appears to be nothing between these high priced cars and the ox cart with its bare-footed attendant. There is practically no middle class between the very rich and the very poor.
>
> From the people with whom I talked I learned that roughly ninety percent of the wealth of the country is held by about one half of one percent of the population. Thirty or forty families own nearly everything in the country. They live in almost regal splendor with many attendants, send their children to Europe or the United States to be educated, and spend money lavishly (on themselves). The rest of the population has practically nothing.
>
> I imagine the situation in El Salvador today is very much like France was before the revolution, Russia before its revolution, Mexico before its revolution. . . . A socialistic or communistic revolution in El Salvador may be delayed for several years, ten or even twenty, but when it comes, it will be a bloody one.

The major was right on all counts but one. The bloodshed was only one month away.

Born in the years when Theodore Roosevelt was still perfecting his "big stick" policy for Central America, Vicky Martínez's father, Lucas, came from a peasant family that farmed in the foothills of the Guzapa Volcano north of San Salvador. Lucas attended a school through the fourth grade, which made him an educated man in a country where, as late as 1967, only one in five children completed the primary grades.

Lucas began picking coffee on the nearby *fincas* when he was still a boy. By 1932, at the age of thirty, his education and experienced had landed him a job as a bookkeeper on a plantation a few miles from the city of Santa Tecla. The plantation belonged to Benjamín Sol Millett, a member of one of the fourteen families. The two men were close in age. Sol Millett appreciated the bookkeeper's hard work and intelligence. They became fast friends.

During the 1920s, coffee production had expanded rapidly. By the end of the decade, it accounted for more than 90 percent of the country's exports. These were happy times for the oligarchy, which wasn't overly concerned that, because vast stretches of El Salvador were planted in coffee, the country had to import basic foods.

Then came the Wall Street stock market crash. Coffee prices collapsed with it. By 1931, they had been cut in half. Wages for *finca* workers dropped from about 50 centavos a day to 20. Work that paid even that much was hard to find. With prices so low, many growers had decided to let their crop rot in the field.

At the same time, the large landowners with some money in reserve used the time to gain control of the land of hundreds of smaller farmers who were in a less-favorable position to weather the bad times. More than a quarter of all land changed hands during the first year of the Depression.

Unemployment rose to 40 percent among the rural work force. The result was labor unrest in the coffee-producing regions, even though rural workers still were not legally permitted to organize. The labor movement had begun gaining strength in the cities during World War I. It took on a more militant tone with arrival of radical organizers from Mexico and Guatemala during the early 1920s. By the time of the Depression, unions in the west had signed up eighty thousand.

In April 1930, fifty thousand people signed a petition demanding that labor laws cover farm workers and guarantee a minimum wage. The following month, the country's fledgling Communist party led eighty thousand people in a march on San Salvador, which at the time had a population of only ninety thousand.

The party's best-known organizer was Augustín Farabundo Martí. Martí, born in 1893 to a wealthy landowner from La Libertad, studied law for a time at the National University in San Salvador before quitting to devote himself to political work. Because of his Marxist activities, he was thrown out of the country in 1920. After helping to form a socialist party in Guatemala City, he returned to El Salvador in 1925. His political organizing among workers and students got him thrown into jail, where he began a well-publicized hunger strike. The resulting uproar from labor unions and university students forced the government to release him.

This time, he left the country on his own and briefly joined Augusto Sandino, the guerrilla fighter then waging a war against the Somoza regime and U.S. Marines in Nicaragua. He returned to El Salvador again in 1930, at a time when hundreds of students and workers were being arrested for taking part in demonstrations and strikes. Martí quickly found himself among them, although, after another long hunger strike, he was once again freed.

Martí and other leftist organizers began working quietly among peasants in the coffee-growing regions. The Marxists became especially strong in western El Salvador, so strong that legislative and municipal elections were suspended in some towns in early January 1932. In areas where the Communists won, the military government refused to let their candidates take office. With that, Martí and his followers began making plans for a revolution.

Four days before the uprising was to begin, Martí was captured by police. Although their plans had been uncovered, the other leaders of the revolt did not get word to their followers in the west. On the night of January 22, 1932, thousands of peasants, most of them Indians, came down from the mountains. Armed mostly with machetes, they overran five small towns, looting stores, burning homes, attacking government offices, and, in a few cases, hacking prominent citizens to death.

When a mob took over the *finca* where Lucas Martínez was working, he fled into the countryside knowing that, even as a bookkeeper for the Sol Millett family, he was a target. As he made his way toward Santa Tecla, Lucas could see buildings burning and more mobs moving down the roads. One day, from his hiding place, he watched as they captured one man, tied him up, and then murdered him. There was madness all around.

By the time Lucas reached Santa Tecla, government troops were moving into the countryside to quash the rebellion. By January 25, it was all but over. In his 1971 study of the revolt, historian Thomas P. Anderson estimates that as many as one hundred — civilians, police, and soldiers — were killed by the rebels during the three-day uprising. Then the real slaughter began.

Gen. Maximiliano Hernández Martínez, who had become president as a result of a coup a few weeks earlier, ordered the security forces to round up the leaders of the rebellion. Because of his taste for the occult, Hernández Martínez was known among his countrymen as "El Brujo," the warlock. Among other things, as Anderson reports, Hernández Martínez believed it was a greater crime to kill an ant than a man. An ant died forever; a human being would be reincarnated. During the weeks following the rebellion, Hernández Martínez put thousands of men, women, and children on the road to reincarnation. Anyone with Indian features became suspect. So were those who wore Indian dress or carried a machete, the traditional work tool of the *campesinos*. In many areas, people who had not taken part in the rebellion were told to report to the local military commander to receive safe conduct papers. At Asunción, Juayua, Nahuizalco, and other towns, the applicants were tied together by their thumbs and put before firing squads. Some were first marched into the town square and ordered to dig their own graves. In the capital, the military reviewed voting lists and arrested anyone who had cast a ballot for the Communist party. For days, hundreds of suspects were trucked to a nearby river and shot.

Estimates vary on how many people were murdered in the

aftermath of the rebellion. Some put the figure as high as thirty thousand. Anderson believes it was closer to ten thousand. Salvadorans generations later would still refer to it as "La Matanza," the massacre.

Hernández Martínez managed to maintain power for twelve years. After wiping out peasant opposition in the Matanza, he banned labor unions and peasant organizations and discouraged opposition political parties, all this in keeping with his growing admiration for the European fascists.

Hernández Martínez also installed his military cronies in most positions of power, a move that frustrated the ambitions of many younger officers. By 1944, the general also faced opposition from other quarters. The growing professional class — doctors, lawyers, professors, and engineers — grumbled over its lack of political power. Even elements of the oligarchy were tired of the general's refusal to wean the economy from its dependence on coffee. In April, there was an attempted coup. Hernández Martínez executed the conspirators, but within days a general strike paralyzed the economy. Within a few weeks the old general fled to Honduras.

The new provisional president, Gen. Andrés Ignacio Menéndez, included politicians of all stripes in his cabinet. He also released political prisoners, encouraged freedom of the press, and abolished the secret police. But coupled with the rise of new political parties, Menéndez's talk of free elections was too much for the conservatives to fathom, and so, five months after he took office, he was overthrown in another coup.

Salvadorans would see the same cycle repeated again and again for the next forty years. Public unrest would be followed by brief respites of modest economic and social reform that would inevitably end in a military coup and more repression. Meanwhile, the problems of the peasantry were never addressed and the frustrations of the middle class continued to fester. Only the oligarchy prospered through it all.

In addition to their coffee *fincas,* the Sol Millett family ran finance companies, sold agricultural machinery, and operated an

urban housing project. One of its most celebrated holdings was
a combination cattle ranch and coconut plantation that occupied
an entire island in the Bay of Jiquilisco. Six miles long and three
wide, Espíritu Santo, was home for twelve hundred Sol Millet
employees. Although the workers were paid comparatively well,
every aspect of their daily lives — including access to the mainland — was controlled by the family. The family maintained a
huge mansion on the property, along with a yacht and a small
landing strip.

For several years after the Matanza, Lucas Martínez lived and
worked on Espíritu Santo. Years later Sol Millett offered him a
job as a foreman at his five-thousand-acre *finca* near Colón, a
small town about fifteen miles west of San Salvador. Sol Millett
had built a coffee-processing plant there and he wanted his old
and trusted friend to help oversee the operation.

At the *finca*, Lucas married Kathalina, who was thirty years
younger than he. Before meeting him, she and her two sisters
worked spreading fertilizer on the *finca*. Lucas and his new bride
moved into a whitewashed four-bedroom house near the plantation office and began to raise a family. Ernesto was born in 1957.
Then came Corina, Vicky, and Isaiahs.

Although her husband's salary was sufficient for the family to
live a comfortable life, Kathalina never stopped working. When
she was not taking care of the children, she baked bread and made
food to sell to the workers. Lucas, then approaching sixty, spent
his days tending the plants, poring over the ledgers, and walking
to distant parts of the plantation to oversee the workers. He and
Benjamín Sol Millett remained close. At Christmas time, the
plantation owner gave Lucas wristwatches and other expensive
gifts. Eventually, he bought Lucas a horse.

The children began picking coffee when they were very young,
but unlike the sons and daughters of the *colonos* and seasonal
workers, it was not out of necessity. They used the money to buy
notebooks, pencils, and school clothes. Lucas and Kathalina
wanted all their children to be educated. When they had completed the primary grades at the small plantation school, the
couple somehow found tuition money to send them to secondary
and trade schools. Ernesto, Corina, Vicky, and Isaiahs went, but

like students all over the country in the early 1970s, they learned
more than their parents expected.

As the 1972 elections approached, Fidel Sánchez Hernández,
El Salvador's latest general-turned-president, began to lose support among the oligarchy's radical right wing. Even Sánchez Hernández's hollow talk about land reform frightened them. Instead
of supporting his handpicked successor, Col. Arturo Molina, the
oligarchy nominated its own candidate, Gen. José Alberto
Medrano, former director of the National Guard and founder of
ORDEN, a rural vigilante group that drew few boundaries in its
war against the Left.

But the real campaign was between Molina, candidate of
the Party of National Conciliation (PCN), and José Napoleón
Duarte, the popular former mayor of San Salvador, where about
30 percent of the nation's voters lived. Duarte was one of the
founders of the Christian Democratic party (PDC) in El Salvador. With its platform of social and economic reform and the
support of the United States, the PDC had had great success in
local and legislative elections during the 1960s.

For the 1972 presidential elections, it bolstered its support by
forming the National Opposition Union (UNO) with two smaller
parties: the National Democratic Union (UDN) included members of the outlawed Communist party; the Revolutionary
National Movement (MNR) was a member of the Socialist International. Both were further to the left than the PDC. Duarte
chose the MNR secretary-general, attorney Guillermo Manuel
Ungo, as his running mate.

Duarte visited more than two hundred towns during the three-
month campaign. In the style of a North American politician, he
shook hands, walked among the voters, and gave long but rousing
speeches about his plans to institute agrarian reform, promote in-
dustrialization, and return the country to true democracy.

Molina's supporters attacked the UNO candidates as Communists, but the colonel himself did little campaigning outside the
major cities and towns. He was relying on his party's powerful organization to carry the election for him, which it ultimately did.

The first returns came from the rural areas, where the PCN controlled the ballot boxes. They gave Molina the lead for a time, but then results from San Salvador pushed the UNO slate ahead. At that point, the PCN-dominated Federal Elections Board stopped announcing results. The next day, the board declared Molina the winner by twenty-two thousand votes, although, because of the votes for the smaller parties, he did not get the majority needed to become president. Amid cries of fraud from Duarte's supporters, the election was thrown into the National Assembly, another bastion of PCN power. To no one's surprise, the vote there went to Molina.

Duarte was not ready to challenge the outcome, but some young military officers were. On the morning of March 25, they revolted, arresting Sánchez Hernández and occupying the Zapote Barracks, located on a hillside above the Presidential Palace. The rebellion did not gain support in the provinces, however, and within hours, loyalist columns began to converge on the capital. After some hesitation, Duarte went on national radio and urged his followers to spread nails across the highways to stall the advancing troops.

It was too late and too little. Even as he spoke, the rebellion was crumbling. In the bloodshed that followed, more than one hundred people died. Duarte was arrested, beaten, and put on a plane to Guatemala. The stolen election sapped the strength of the political center, leaving radicals on the left and right to vie for power.

After his inauguration that July, Molina vowed to wipe the country clean of communism. His first target was the University of El Salvador. Troops, tanks, and helicopters moved in to shut down the school. Hundreds of professors and students were arrested. The university president and the medical school dean were exiled. The university had been home base for many radical leftists, but coupled with the stolen election, Molina's overkill only succeeded in bringing more Salvadorans to their cause.

Cayetano Carpio, then fifty-two, was among the oldest of the revolutionaries. A labor leader, he had gone on to become head of the Communist party. While pushing for radical change in El Salvador, the party had traditionally opposed armed revolution.

Disillusioned with such a strategy, Carpio and a few followers had gone underground in 1970 and formed the Popular Liberation Forces (FPL). Although the FPL aimed at armed insurrection, Carpio and his followers also stressed the need to build political bases among the people.

The other guerrilla group that formed in those years, the Revolutionary Army of the People (ERP), was even more militaristic. Composed of younger Communists and Christian Democrats, the ERP made armed struggle its primary goal. To finance its cause, it kidnapped wealthy Salvadorans and foreign businessmen and held them for huge ransoms. Within the ERP, however, there were also those who believed political organizing among the peasants was important. The most prominent among them was poet Roque Dalton, who had spent years studying in Chile, Cuba, and other countries before returning to El Salvador.

It was Dalton who, using another name, began to visit the *finca* where the Martínez family lived.

With the revolutionaries organizing in the countryside, Sol Millett arranged for a small detachment of National Guardsmen to be stationed on the *finca*. They warned Lucas Martínez and the other foremen to be on the lookout for subversives who were agitating among coffee workers in the area. Several times a week, they came to Lucas's home to question him about individual workers and people in the nearby village. They also wanted to know about any strangers he had seen passing through.

Lucas always promised to be vigilant, but he never turned anyone in. The security forces had other spies among the people who did. Those denounced as subversives were dealt with quickly. One suspected organizer from the village was kidnapped one night. He was found, near death, beside a river a few days later. Others guilty of lesser infractions such as discussing workers' rights or higher pay at the village water pump, were simply fired from their jobs and blacklisted from further employment.

Although Lucas did not know it at first, the seeds of revolution had been planted within his own family. Like so many young people in El Salvador, his oldest son, Ernesto, was among those who believed it was time for radical change.

On the *finca*, Ernesto had listened to the workers grousing about their low pay and lack of rights. After one friend, a member of the local soccer team, had his foot cut off in a tractor accident, the *finca* refused to give him any compensation.

Ernesto's concerns were only reinforced at the high school, where a few of his teachers challenged the students to think about the inequalities between the rich and poor in El Salvador. Ernesto had been there the day teachers across the country called their first strike. In a show of solidarity, Ernesto and the other students barricaded themselves inside the building until a detachment of soliders came to roust them. While no one was hurt in the demonstration, it was a sign of things to come.

Despite his father's warnings, Ernesto became more and more involved with the opposition. He met the organizers who passed through the *finca*, sometimes persuading Lucas, who did not know their identity, to allow them to sleep at the family's home. Roque Dalton came several times, although it was not until years later, after he saw pictures of the poet in the United States, that Ernesto knew the man's true identity. At night, they would gather interested workers and walk deep into the coffee fields to talk. Often, they met in the pouring rain.

Ernesto sympathized with the ERP's goals, but he did not like their military posture. He, like Dalton, believed that before military action could be successful, the peasants had to be educated and organized.

Although there was never any fighting around the *finca*, the revolution got closer. In late February 1977, Lucas sent his two daughters off to San Salvador to study at a secretarial school. They arrived in the capital just as UNO supporters were protesting the outcome of another election.

The UNO had nominated a retired colonel, Ernesto Claramount, as its presidential candidate. As ballots were being cast, UNO election observers were physically removed from several polling places around the country. The result was that the military-backed candidate, Gen. Carlos Humberto Romero, was declared the winner by a three-to-one margin.

Claramount and several hundred of his supporters crowded

into Plaza Libertad in downtown San Salvador. They stayed there for days, listening to Claramount condemn the results and demand a new election. The crowd had grown to about fifty thousand when early on the morning of February 28, truckloads of soldiers and police arrived. After blocking all but one entrance to the plaza, they opened fire. Ninety people were shot, about half of them fatally, as Claramount and several hundred supporters ran for cover.

The school Corina and Vicky Martínez were to attend was located on the plaza. They arrived for their first day of class the morning after the shootings. Although the blood had been hosed away, the two sisters found their way blocked by troops.

Later that year, Benjamín Sol Millett was kidnapped by the guerrillas and released only after his family paid a huge ransom. Lucas Martínez's old friend returned from the ordeal a sick and broken man and soon turned the business over to his son.

The growing unrest at the *finca* only added to Lucas Martínez's frustration. During the harvest, he had always hired extra workers. Many came from the departments of Morazán in the east, and Chalatenango in the north. By 1977, leftists had been organizing in both areas. So had a new breed of activist priests, who urged peasants to stand up for their rights. The workers who came to the *finca* that year were no longer the docile people Lucas had known for so many years.

They demanded more than the small ration of tortillas and beans the *finca* had given them in the past. One day, they surrounded a trailer filled with coffee beans and threatened to push it over unless they were given enough food for their children. Another afternoon, a group of workers confronted Lucas in a dispute over the weight of the beans they had picked. Finally, as the workers were leaving the *finca* after the harvest, some of them chopped down an acre or so of coffee plants with their machetes.

Lucas, then approaching eighty, was tired of it all. He asked the Sol Millets for his retirement settlement and made plans to leave the *finca*. With some of the money, he sent Ernesto to the nearby city of Armenia to buy a small plot of land and build the family a new home. Ernesto found a lot in a barrio close to town and rented a few acres nearby so that the family could grow corn and beans.

Ernesto had, by then, lost contact with Roque Dalton, who had been denounced as a CIA spy and executed by more militant rivals within the ERP. For more than a year, Ernesto forgot about politics and concentrated on resettling his family. He was, after all, the oldest son.

Like most Salvadorans, the Martínez family had always been good Catholics, but the parish priest in Armenia preached a gospel that was vastly different from the one they had heard in the old village. The priest there had counseled his people to be patient, respect authority, and accept their place on earth. In contrast, the priest in Armenia stood before his congregation each Sunday and denounced the military's violence and called for justice for the poor.

Church members had formed "Christian base communities" within the parish. These were small groups of one or two dozen people who got together regularly to pray, study the Bible, and discuss what to do about their everyday problems. From the priest and their lay teachers, members of the base communities learned that God had not put them in this world merely to suffer. In his eyes, they were equal to the generals or the coffee barons. As such, they had a right to organize, strike, and speak out on the course their lives took.

The "liberation theology," as it was called, had its roots in the Second Vatican Council. When it concluded in 1965, the council issued two statements that changed the face of Catholicism in much of Latin America. The council proclaimed that the church should be involved in more than matters of the spirit. What happened in this life was also important. Second, it stated that, through baptism, all members of the church were equal in the eyes of God.

These pronouncements came as quite a shock in El Salvador, where, since the days of the Spanish conquest, the church had always been a conservative institution allied with the interests of the rich and powerful. They also perturbed members of the oligarchy, who thought priests belonged in the church tending to the sacraments.

Their anxiety was not eased when the Latin American bishops

met in Medellín, Colombia, in 1968. Pope Paul VI, who opened the meeting, urged the rich to be "sensitive to the voices crying out for bread, concern, justice, and a more active participation in the direction of society." The bishops called upon the church to become an advocate for the poor. More important, it urged the clergy to help the poor develop the sort of education, organization, and leadership they needed to liberate themselves from poverty.

Although many Salvadoran bishops opposed liberation theology, Archbishop Luis Chávez y González became one of its strongest supporters. So was Oscar Arnulfo Romero, who succeeded him as archbishop in 1977. The Jesuit-run Central American University (UCA) also became a center of the new teachings.

By 1976, the church had established seven centers to train catechists and lay preachers, a necessity in a country where there was only one priest for every ten thousand people. The catechists and lay preachers, elected by members of their base communities, provided leadership among the peasants. In addition to leading their communities in religious studies, they also taught reading, agriculture, and community organizing. In areas like Armenia, the priests joined them.

The Martínez family believed this new message of liberation. Lucas and his wife began holding reading classes at their home. Vicky taught children their catechism.

The generals and millionaires were less than delighted by such religious activity among the peasants. They had maintained power and privilege for generations and had no intention of giving it up. In 1975, a priest from San Vicente was arrested by the National Guard and tortured. By mid-1977, two priests had been murdered and many others had been arrested, tortured, or exiled. Leaflets circulating in the capital called on Salvadorans to "Be a Patriot! Kill a Priest!" In the countryside, leaders of the base communities were singled out for similar treatment.

Archbishop Romero refused to silence his followers. His Sunday homilies, broadcast to the nation via the church radio station, became more and more critical of the regime. At the end of each sermon, he also read the names of all those who had been disappeared or murdered the previous week. Even warnings from

Rome failed to quiet the diminutive archbishop. In February 1980, Romero wrote Jimmy Carter and asked him to end all U.S. military aid to El Salvador. A few weeks later, in a sermon, he appealed to all members of El Salvador's security forces to disobey their commanders when ordered to kill.

The day after that sermon, Romero went to a cancer hospital to say a memorial mass. As he asked those gathered to bow their heads and pray, a gunman appeared in the doorway of the chapel. He silenced the archbishop with a single bullet through the heart.

By then, El Salvador was in the midst of a bloodbath unlike anything it had suffered since the Matanza.

Pres. Carlos Humberto Romero's heavy hand alienated the Carter administration in Washington, which had come into office promising to defend human rights around the world. Even some members of the Salvadoran oligarchy questioned the general's methods. Each atrocity only seemed to attract more people to the leftist cause. By 1979, the so-called mass organizations, which included peasants, students, teachers, and union members, were claiming tens of thousands of members. Even the deadly guns of Romero's soldiers failed to stop their strikes and demonstrations. Although the guerrillas remained small in number, they continued to bomb government installations and kidnap prominent Salvadorans.

In July, the Somoza dictatorship fell in nearby Nicaragua. Hundreds of his troops fled to El Salvador. Watching the events next door, many young Salvadoran officers began to worry that Romero's repression might result in the same fate for them. Within three months, there was yet another coup.

It began early on the morning of October 15, 1979. At military outposts around the country, young officers began arresting their commanders. By nightfall, Romero and his aides were on a plane bound for Guatemala.

The new junta, which included civilians from the political Left and Center, pledged to launch a program of social and economic reform. Political prisoners would be freed, ORDEN would be disbanded, and military officers guilty of human rights violations would be punished. Even some of the guerrilla groups agreed to a cease-fire to give the new government a chance.

The brief truce ended at about the same time the new government began to unravel. The young officers dismissed or forced into retirement about one hundred right-wing army and police commanders, but the move was not enough to break the security forces of their old habits.

Three hundred political prisoners who were to be released suddenly disappeared from jail cells. While conservatives within the military and the various police forces frustrated any move toward reform, troops continued to fire on demonstrators and strikers. During the first three weeks of the junta, more than one hundred Salvadorans were killed by the security forces, ORDEN, or the right-wing death squads.

Progressives within the junta demanded that the military high command stop the killings. When their ultimatum was ignored, most of them resigned from the new government. Several went on to form the Democratic Revolutionary Front (FDR), which, with its military arm, the Farabundo Martí National Liberation Front (FMLN), began laying plans for a full-scale revolution. The junta, in the meantime, persuaded a few Christian Democrats to join in order to preserve at least a façade of legitimacy.

But the killing continued. On January 22, 1979, two hundred thousand people marched through San Salvador to commemorate the 1932 Matanza. It was a peaceful demonstration until the marchers reached the plaza outside the National Palace. There, the security forces opened fire. Between twenty and fifty demonstrators were killed, more than one hundred were wounded.

In February, Attorney General Mario Zamora, a Christian Democrat, suggested that his party needed to negotiate with the popular organizations. Zamora, who had also been investigating the disappearance of the three hundred political prisoners, was denounced as a Communist by Roberto D'Aubuisson, a former army intelligence officer who headed up a paramilitary band known as the White Warriors Union. Two days later, gunmen burst into Zamora's home and executed him.

During the first ten weeks of 1980, the Salvadoran Human Rights Commission recorded 689 political murders. The toll took

a big jump a few weeks later when 40 people were killed at Archbishop Romero's funeral.

Five boys from Vicky Martínez's school class disappeared in
the months that followed. So did three of the other catechists in
Armenia. Eventually, the security forces picked up the parish
priest for questioning. After three days of torture, he was
released. Fearing he would not be so lucky next time, the priest
fled to Mexico.

By then, Ernesto had become a leading organizer for the 28th
of February Popular Leagues (LP-28), an opposition group
formed by National University students and named to commemorate the 1977 massacre at Plaza Libertad. He formed small cells
of collaborators within his barrio and recruited other organizers
to work in the surrounding neighborhoods. Ernesto also sent
Vicky and his younger brother Isaiahs to school with propaganda
leaflets, which they quietly distributed. To avoid arrest, he
seldom slept at home. His father supported what Ernesto was
doing, although he worried constantly. His mother cried knowing
that it was only a matter of time before the security forces caught
up with her son.

By January 1981, the FDR-FMLN had launched a "final offensive," which, although unsuccessful in toppling the government,
did result in several departments' falling under rebel control. As
the fighting continued, the security forces intensified their hunt
for subversives.

Vicky Martínez's boyfriend was arrested at Santa Tecla. At
about the same time, a young cousin of Kathalina's was picked up
near Sonsonate. Both had visited Lucas's home and both, as
Ernesto knew, were organizers for the opposition.

The troops came for Lucas Martínez and his family late one
afternoon in May 1981. Along with Vicky and Isaiahs, Ernesto
and his young son, Luis, were at home when neighbors rushed in
to tell them that the National Guard had surrounded the entire
barrio. They went outside to see soldiers making house-to-house
searches up the street.

Lucas and his wife decided to wait for them, believing that the

Guard would not harm them because of their age. Ernesto and the others fled into the countryside. He and his brother made their way to his in-laws' home. Vicky and Luis went to stay with some other relatives.

Lucas and his wife soon found that they had guessed wrong about the Guard's intentions. The soldiers entered their house and began to ransack it. They found an old Air Force shirt that Ernesto's cousin had given him. This, they told Lucas, was the uniform of a guerrilla. Then they noticed the framed photograph of Archbishop Romero. Only a subversive would hang such a thing in his house, they said before taking the couple off for questioning.

The interrogation lasted for eight days. During that time, they accused Lucas of being a subversive and demanded to know the organizations and people with whom he worked. During one session, Lucas's wife was forced to watch while her elderly husband was beaten with fists and rifle butts.

Stories about the arrest appeared in the San Salvador press. They said the security forces had uncovered a guerrilla safe house. The picture showed the old man carrying a rifle through his neighborhood. The authorities returned to the family home after the pictures were taken. After ransacking it, they burned it to the ground. An armed guard was posted at the site.

Over the objections of the authorities, a judge released Lucas and Kathalina. After reuniting with Vicky and Luis, they made their way to a highway and caught a bus for Usulután, a department in the eastern part of the country. Lucas's son from his first marriage lived there.

Lucas and his family hid there for three months until a threatening letter arrived from the local police. Years later, Ernesto would come to suspect that the letter had actually been written by his step-brother, who probably feared the security forces might find out that he was shielding the family. At any rate, within hours of receiving the letter they were once again in flight.

They met up with Ernesto and Isaiahs at a *finca* near Santa Ana. A cousin worked there. They lived with her, worked in the fields, and tried to decide what to do next. All agreed that they could not remain on the *finca* long without being discovered.

ORDEN spies were everywhere. Their only choice was to leave El Salvador.

With his home and savings gone, Lucas told his sons he was too old to support the family outside the country. Isaiahs was determined to remain in El Salvador. With all that had happened to his family, he had decided to go up into the mountains and join the guerrillas. Ernesto wanted to continue organizing, but he felt responsible for the family. It was his work that had made them targets.

Ernesto went to Mexico, hoping to find work and a place for the family to live. He wandered across the Guatemalan border into a labor camp for a road construction crew. The boss there gave him a job working on one of the big earthmovers. Within a few weeks, he began sending money back to his family along with instructions on the best way to travel through Guatemala and on to Mexico.

After buying false identity papers, Lucas and his family got visitor's visas and took a bus to Guatemala City. The next day, they rode another toward the frontier. That night they floated across the Río Suciate on inner tubes. Ernesto and some Mexican friends were waiting on the other side.

For a time, they lived near the work camp in a small hut Ernesto had built of sticks and palm leaves. When he was promoted to the company's payroll office in nearby Tapachula, the family went with him. There, a priest told them they could stay in the courtyard behind his church. The shelter there had no wall or floor, but at least there was a roof over their heads and a place to tie up their hammocks.

Soon more refugees began to arrive. One of them was a young army deserter from Guatemala. He too was on the run.

4

Guatemala: A Soldier's Story

Until that day in the summer of 1979, Rodrigo García never questioned orders. The young corporal, picked up by a troop truck one night as he hitchhiked down a rural highway, had been forced into the Guatemalan Army. But he had grown fond of the military life. The army provided food, clothing, and a paycheck, which was better than he had done for himself as a civilian. Rodrigo had finally begun to feel that perhaps life could be better than it had been for his father, a man who had always spoken as if life were one long, dark test of endurance and pain. The army gave Rodrigo a sense of belonging and mission. Moreover, women seemed captivated by his dark uniform and tough military bearing.

After basic training and a few weeks of heavy weapons instruction, Rodrigo was assigned to a small garrison a few kilometers from the Salvadoran border. He and about thirty other soldiers stationed there patrolled the nearby farms and plantations. They also stopped traffic on the Pan-American Highway, emptying the cars and buses to check the documents of travelers coming into Guatemala. The Salvadoran boys trying to sneak into the country without papers were sometimes roughed up a bit before being sent back across the border. Rodrigo and his comrades wanted to let them know who was in charge on the Guatemalan side.

The base itself was located on the edge of a large plantation. The owner gave them fresh fruit and meat. The soldiers also rode his horses while on patrol. The base was a blessing for the wealthy landowner. In addition to protecting his cattle and orchards from guerrilla attacks, the soldiers also made the local peasants think long and hard before they got involved with labor unions or some other "subversive" activity.

One summer afternoon, the landowner and the lieutenant in charge of the base drove up in the landowner's pickup. In the truck bed lay a young man. He was gagged and bound. Probably a subversive, Rodrigo thought, as soldiers dragged the prisoner to the tiny guardhouse beside the highway. He was dressed too well to be a peasant, and the commander never made such a fuss over drunks or cattle thieves. The soldiers spent the rest of the afternoon taunting and beating the prisoner as he cowered inside the guardhouse.

Just after 10 P.M., the lieutenant ordered Rodrigo and four other soldiers to get their rifles and report to the pickup truck. They threw the prisoner back onto the truck bed and climbed in with him. The landowner and the lieutenant got into the cab and they drove to an isolated stretch of road.

"I need two of you here," the lieutenant said as his men climbed down from the truck. "Which of you has more balls?"

Two soldiers stepped forward. The lieutenant gave his pistol to the fat one everybody called "El Pollo," the chicken. The soldiers untied the prisoner's feet and marched him into the brush. From the darkness, Rodrigo heard the prisoner's voice for the first time. The man screamed that the soldiers were assassins. Then he shouted something about one of the guerrilla groups. One day they would win, he said. Two shots rang out.

After El Pollo and the other soldier returned to the truck, the lieutenant gathered his men around him. "You know," he warned, "in this kind of work, you have to be quiet."

As they drove back to the base, El Pollo proudly told Rodrigo that he had fired the shots. "These sons of bitches," El Pollo said, "we have to kill them."

For the first time, the corporal began to wonder.

Rodrigo had spent most of his childhood in and around Guatemala City, moving from house to house as his father's fortunes rose and fell. Arturo García sold insurance. At times, he earned an adequate living. Other years, there was no work. Arturo was a short, rough-hewn man with dark brown skin and eyes that were black as peat. On Saturday afternoon, he and his cronies usually got together for pool or dominoes. They would drink, joke, and wisecrack for hours. But at home, Arturo was a distant, almost melancholy man who sat shirtless beside his ancient short-wave radio and pored over the newspapers. Arturo rarely told his children fairy tales or bedtime stories. Years later, Rodrigo, the fifth of eight children, would remember his father as a man who usually spoke of how hard and ugly life was for the poor.

Arturo had grown up in El Salvador, the son of a peasant family from outside the city of Santa Ana in the western part of the country. A yellow fever epidemic killed his parents when he was thirteen. He lived with an uncle for a few years, then moved to San Salvador, the capital, where he shined shoes. By eighteen, Arturo had saved enough money to buy his own ice cream cart. But the Great Depression had destroyed the international demand for coffee, the main money crop for the already-poor country. On the great plantations, landowners were letting their crops rot in the field. Amid the resulting poverty and unemployment, a man could not earn a decent living selling frozen treats.

But, poor as he was, at least Arturo was better off than the peasants back home. They were being slaughtered in the Matanza.

Arturo García paid little attention to politics in those days. After giving up on his ice cream business, he roamed through other Central American countries, looking for a better life. He even slipped into the United States for a short time and found a job clearing snow from railroad tracks.

Years later, Arturo would tell his son Rodrigo one story from those years over and over again. He and another man were in Panama. They had been hired to burn garbage at a dump near the Canal Zone. Much of it came from the American families who lived nearby. Arturo was always careful to rummage through their trash before burning it. The Americans threw away amazing things.

One day, Arturo and his friend found a full bottle of American whiskey. As the two men were enjoying their treasure, a big, well-dressed American walked up and offered them a job taking care of his yard. Even as an old man, Arturo would still recall what a big house the American had, full of food and fine furniture. What was life that the Americans could have so much while he, Arturo, worked so hard for so little? As the years passed, Arturo's envy turned to anger and then hate.

Rodrigo could never understand how his mother and father had fallen in love. They were so different. His mother, Estella, was a tall, fair-skinned woman with cool green eyes and light brown hair. Although she died when Rodrigo was only twelve, he remembered her as a woman with an educated, almost elegant air. Estella was the illegitimate daughter of a Salvadoran woman and a rich Spaniard. She had been raised by her grandmother, a relatively wealthy woman who sent Estella to the best church schools. At the age of fifteen, Estella was already earning good pay as a secretary in San Salvador.

Even after she married Arturo in 1944 and began raising her children, Estrella continued to write poems and short stories. But life was not easy for the young Salvadoran family and money was not the only reason. Arturo was a maintenance man at a bank then but he had previously worked as a baker. Through that job, he had gotten involved in union organizing, a dangerous and often fatal endeavor in 1940s El Salvador.

Through the late 1940s, the unions continued to organize and strike. In 1946, the bakers' union along with some textile workers tried to launch a general strike aimed at toppling the government. This one was unsuccessful and more than two hundred participants were arrested. By 1951, many labor leaders had either been exiled or imprisoned. Others went into hiding.

Arturo García moved his family from one home to the next, trying to elude the police, but eventually he was captured and thrown into prison with the others. They remained behind bars until Guatemala offered them asylum.

Ten years earlier, the offer could not have been proffered. Guatemala had its own dictator then, one who, like General Hernández Martínez, believed in the politics of blood. But Guatemala had changed and, even as an old man, Arturo would remember the day he and the other union leaders had arrived there. He would proudly tell his son Rodrigo that Jacobo Arbenz, the president of Guatemala, had come to welcome their train.

Roughly the size of Ohio, Guatemala is a land of stunning beauty. A volcano-studded chain of mountains stretches from its northwest border with Mexico nearly to the Salvadoran frontier in the southeast. Between its rugged peaks lie dozens of deep, isolated valleys, fertile plateaus, and clear volcanic lakes, which sustain descendants of the Mayan Indians who once ruled the area.

To the northeast, the lands slopes gently toward the tropical lowlands along the Caribbean coast. Due north lie the swamps and jungles of the sparsely populated region known as El Petén. To the south and west, the highlands give way to some of the richest soil in all of Central America. The piedmont area supports the nation's vast coffee plantations. Corn, cotton, and sugar cane are grown on the Pacific coastal plain. The land is also used to graze cattle.

Guatemala is one of the wealthiest and most powerful nations in Central America. But since the Spanish conquest, it has also endured one of the bloodiest histories in the region. Spaniards under Don Pedro de Alvarado defeated the Maya in the 1520s. The Indians did not accept the conquest passively, but the Spaniards used their superior weaponry to crush subsequent revolts with brutal efficiency. European diseases such as measles and smallpox further decimated the indigenous population.

Although the Spanish government outlawed Indian slavery in 1541, it instituted other measures that continued to disrupt the native culture. The crown doled out land to its servants and gave them the power to extract tribute — crops, labor, or gold — from the Indians who had lived on it for centuries. In the villages, Indians were forced to donate their labor to colonial officials and landowners. Some retreated deeper into the highlands to avoid the Spanish demands, but in 1543, the government began rounding them up and forcing them into centralized villages, ostensibly so that the church could more easily convert them to Christianity.

The result was that even more Indian land was claimed for the colonists' haciendas.

In some areas, the Indians were able to maintain their culture and religion, and with them a deep suspicion of outsiders. They were not the only ones dissatisfied with the Spaniards and their New World descendants, however. Unions between colonists and Indians had produced a growing number of "Ladinos," who were shunned by both societies. By the nineteenth century, Ladinos and Indians accounted for all but a small percentage of the population of Guatemala.

After independence from Spain in 1821, there were brief periods of reform, but for the most part, the basic profile of Guatemalan society remained the same. A small group of wealthy men controlled the country's land and wealth. They maintained their power with the help of a long line of right-wing generals and strongmen who ruled the government. The peasants, most of them Indians, continued to be plagued by land grabs and forced labor. Any uprisings were quickly stomped out by Guatemalan troops.

Guatemala's fertile land, cheap labor, and strict government control made it attractive to foreign investors. By the early twentieth century, German investors owned much of the land used to grow coffee. By the 1930s, a single U.S. firm—United Fruit Company—had become Guatemala's largest employer and landowner. In addition to its plantations on the Atlantic and Pacific coasts, the company also owned Guatemala's railroad and communications network and the country's only Atlantic port, Puerto Barrios.

One of United Fruit Company's biggest assets was Gen. Jorge Ubico, who came to power in 1931. The son of a rich coffee grower, Ubico exempted the company from most taxes and import fees and encouraged it to pay workers on its banana plantations no more than fifty cents a day.

The general built schools, roads, and airports for Guatemala, although he required peasants to "donate" their labor for much of the work. Protests were brief and bloody, as Ubico routinely had opponents jailed or murdered. He banned all unions and even forbid the use of words such as "laborer" and "strike."

By 1944, Ubico's support had disappeared among all but the wealthiest of Guatemalans. The urban middle class — merchants, professionals, and government bureaucrats — grew tired of his heavy hand. On their shortwave radios, they, along with many young army officers, had heard the North American president, Franklin Delano Roosevelt, talk about freedom of speech and religion and freedom from want and fear. Closer to home, Pres. Lázaro Cárdenas of Mexico had encouraged his country's labor movement and instituted agricultural reform laws.

Guatemala's teachers were the first to strike. They were quickly joined by others. The demonstrations culminated in a huge march on the capital on June 29, 1944. Ubico's cavalry rode in and killed more than two hundred demonstrators, but the unrest continued and the dictator soon stepped down. Another general attempted to continue the tradition of military rule, but by October, he too had been overthrown.

That December, Guatemalans experienced the most honest election in their history. The winner, with more than 85 percent of the vote, was Juan José Arévalo, a forty-four-year-old philosophy professor who had returned from exile in Argentina. With the public behind him, the new leader immediately set out to build a new society from the ruins of the dictatorship.

One of its elements was a new constitution designed to nurture democracy in Guatemala. The constitution limited the president to one six-year term and prohibited military men from seeking office. In addition to strengthening the legislative and judicial branches of government, it also guaranteed freedom of the press, gave citizens the right to form political parties, and banned discrimination because of sex or race.

Although he did not possess the political acumen to put all of his plans into action, during his six years as president, Arévalo initiated the nation's first social security law, required landowners to rent unused acreage to peasant farmers, and permitted most urban workers to organize and strike.

The oligarchy along with foreign investors such as the United Fruit Company grumbled and, amid the Cold War frenzy of the day, J. Edgar Hoover and the FBI were soon looking for Communists behind the reforms. Although Arévalo personally opposed Marxism, in the face of stubborn opposition from the right he did rely on leftists within the union movement to support his programs.

Under Arévalo, wages for urban workers increased by 80 percent, but rural peasants — who made up 90 percent of Guatemala's work force — were not so lucky. By the end of Arévalo's term, their per capita income remained at around $87 a year. Less than 3 percent of the nation's people maintained control of over 70 percent of its arable land and cultivated less than a quarter of it. The task of agricultural reform fell to Arévalo's successor, Jacobo Arbenz Guzmán.

After taking office in 1951, the handsome ex-Army officer announced his intention to convert Guatemala into a modern capitalist state and raise the standard of living of the people.

The centerpiece of this effort was the agricultural reform bill he steered through the Congress in 1952. It empowered the government to take over uncultivated portions of the large plantations and parcel them out among the peasants. The landowners would be compensated with government bonds. During the next year and a half, 1.5 million acres were distributed, including 1,700 acres belonging to the president.

By 1953, the United Fruit Company (UFCO) owned about 550,000 acres in Guatemala, although only about 15 percent of it was under cultivation. The Arbenz government expropriated 209,000 acres of the unused land and proposed to pay the company $627,000 in bonds for the property. Arbenz based his offer on UFCO's own estimates of the land's worth. For years, UFCO had undervalued its land in order to lower its already minimal tax bills. Suddenly, via the U.S. State Department, UFCO informed Arbenz that the land was worth nearly $16 million. The Guatemalan government responded by expropriating even more acreage in the months that followed.

Arbenz was challenging UFCO domination in other ways as well. He began building a highway to the Atlantic coast, a move that would end Guatemala's dependence on the UFCO railroad. The new president also announced plans for a new, publicly owned port facility that would compete for trade with UFCO facilities at Puerto Barrios.

But United Fruit was far from beaten. The company flew U.S. newsmen to Guatemala to tour its facilities. The result was a spate of favorable stories that cast UFCO as an underdog standing up to communism in Latin America.

The company also began calling on its powerful friends within the U.S. government including two of the most influential men in the Eisenhower administration. Before John Foster Dulles became secretary of state, his New York law firm had represented UFCO. His brother, CIA chief Allen Dulles, had been on the company's board of trustees. Beyond that, President Eisenhower's secretary was married to an UFCO public relations executive. With their help, UFCO was able to convince American politicians that Arbenz was a reckless man steering Guatemala down the road to communism.

Arbenz had permitted Guatemala Communists to organize political parties. In the years since Ubico's overthrow, they had also become a powerful force in the urban unions. Arbenz welcomed their support and gave them positions within the government. But with only four deputies in the 1953–54 Congress, Communists were the smallest party in the president's ruling coalition and he never appointed one to his cabinet. If Arbenz was a Soviet puppet, his continuing to side with the United States at the United Nations was puzzling.

As the first expropriations of UFCO land were occurring in Guatemala, the company's lobbying campaign was succeeding in Washington. The U.S. government made diplomatic attacks on the Arbenz government while CIA operatives funneled money and small arms to right-wing military officers. On March 29, 1953, rebels overran the provincial capital of Salama and held it for nearly a day before loyal troops crushed the rebellion. Five months after the Salama failure, President Eisenhower gave the CIA permission to organize another coup attempt.

"Operation Success," as it was called, was placed in the hands of Col. Albert Haney, chief of CIA operations in Korea during the war there. His plan included attempts to bribe both military officers and Arbenz himself. When that failed, he began planning his revolution in earnest.

With the blessing of Nicaraguan dictator Anastasio Somoza

García, Haney's men established a training camp near Managua
for about 150 men, which included Guatemalan exiles and mer-
cenaries from the United States. Recruiting American pilots, he
also set up an airstrip on Nicaragua's Atlantic coast and began
stocking it with U.S. military planes sneaked in through Nicaragua, Honduras, and the Panama Canal Zone. Haney's propaganda machine included jamming devices and radio transmitters,
including one inside the U.S. Embassy in Guatemala City. Heading up the propaganda war against Arbenz was Howard Hunt,
who nearly two decades later, would become a central figure in
the Watergate scandal.

To lead the "Liberation Army," the CIA chose Col. Carlos
Castillo Armas, a career military man who had unsuccessfully
tried to launch his own rebellion in 1950. On the morning of June
18, 1954, Castillo Armas and about 170 men crossed into Guatemala from Honduras. The attack promptly ground to a halt just
a few miles inside Guatemala, but for the next week CIA pilots
bombed cities, oil depots, and military barracks while the
agency's radio transmitters and propaganda experts worked to
convince Guatemalans that a huge liberation army was bearing
down on the capital.

By Sunday, June 27, frightened Guatemalans were fleeing the
capital and Arbenz had lost the support of his army. At 9:15 that
night, he announced his resignation in a radio broadcast to the
nation. On July 3, Castillo Armas flew into Guatemala City
aboard the U.S. ambassador's plane and took control of the
country.

The new president repaid his North American backers by
revoking the agricultural reform laws, returning the UFCO acreage, and running peasants off the land that had been redistributed
under Arbenz. He also formed a secret committee to track down
supporters of the former president and banned labor unions,
political parties, and peasant organizations. Books were burned,
opponents were shot, the press was censored, and illiterates were
denied the right to vote. Thanks to the CIA, however, American
interests in Guatemala were safe.

Castillo Armas was assassinated in 1957, but the military maintained a tight grip on Guatemalan politics. When a general did

not occupy the National Palace, the army used its power to intimidate and control civilian presidents. Meanwhile, the oligarchy, no longer restrained by the prospect of agricultural reform, dominated the country's economy as it had before the 1944 revolution.

Miguel Ydígoras Fuentes, an old Ubico crony, succeeded Castillo Armas. The elderly general was more talented at finding jobs for his friends and relatives than he was at managing a country. His brother became the ambassador to Washington, his daughter to France. Ydígoras raised his own salary to $150,000, making him the best-paid president in the Western Hemisphere. But he remained one of the Eisenhower administration's most reliable, if inept, friends in Latin America. When the CIA began casting about for a site to train Cuban exiles for the Bay of Pigs invasion, Ydígoras agreed to serve as their host.

Already frustrated by low pay and corruption, some of the army's more nationalistic officers resented the foreign intrusion. On November 13, 1960, they revolted. The rebels seized two garrisons and the Atlantic port of Puerto Barrios before they were defeated by loyalist troops backed by CIA bombers and U.S. Navy patrols. In the months that followed, Ydígoras's security forces rounded up hundreds of rebel soldiers, union members, peasant leaders, and students. Those who were not jailed were shot. A few dissident officers managed to elude capture. They slipped out of Guatemala and joined leftist rebels who had begun plotting their own revolution.

Although inspired by Castro's success in Cuba, the Guatemalan guerrillas of the early 1960s never managed to muster the same level of military might or peasant support. They were easily wiped out by the army and their sympathizers were hunted down. Nevertheless, the leftist activity alarmed Washington.

In hopes of tamping popular support for the insurgency, Pres. John F. Kennedy made Guatemala one of the primary targets of his Alliance for Progress, a program designed to promote democracy through economic growth. Between 1960 and 1966, nearly $50 million in U.S. funds were pumped into the Guatemalan economy, but the money did little to improve the lives of the peasants, who remained among the sickest, hungriest, and least educated people in the Western Hemisphere. The Alliance's chief benefactors were members of the oligarchy, who used U.S. money to pay for projects they might have otherwise financed themselves.

Meanwhile, the Kennedy administration supplied the Guatemalan security forces with modern weapons and training. U.S. Green Berets went to Guatemala to instruct troops in counterinsurgency tactics. Officers of the Guatemalan National Police came to this country for training.

In 1966, the modernized army was unleashed on the guerrillas, who had by then reorganized in the southeastern part of the country. The fighting was most savage in Zacapa Province, where troops under Col. Carlos Arana Osorio wiped out entire villages in his relentless pursuit of the guerrillas and their supporters.

In the cities, thousands more were arrested, tortured, or murdered. Students, labor leaders, and politicians of the Center and Left, in short, anyone who did not side with the right-wing politicians and the military, was a potential target. The state security forces were joined in the grisly crusade by right-wing death squads with names such as the Mano Blanco (the White Hand) and Ojo por Ojo (Eye for an Eye). In December 1967, even Rogelia Cruz Martínez, a former Miss Guatemala, fell victim to one of them.

The guerrillas struck back, murdering U.S. military advisers and, in 1968, U.S. Ambassador John Gordon Mein, but their attacks paled beside those sponsored by the security forces. By 1970, Arana had become president and the military had all but crushed its opposition, but the violence continued. In 1976, Amnesty International estimated that more than twenty thousand Guatemalans had either been murdered or "disappeared" during the previous decade.

After coming to Guatemala in 1944, Arturo García avoided politics and union work. Instead, he settled in Mixco, a small blue-collar town outside Guatemala City, and sold insurance. He still despised the military, the right-wing politicians, and their North American supporters, but he allowed himself to vent his anger only to his family and friends.

A powerful earthquake decimated much of Guatemala in 1976, killing more than twenty thousand people and leaving another million homeless. With the Guatemalan economy in a shambles, Arturo took Rodrigo and four other sons back to El Salvador to search for work.

They settled in Soyapango, a dingy suburb of San Salvador. Some of Rodrigo's older brothers found construction work. The fifteen-year-old got a job pumping gas.

The military government of El Salvador was waging its own war on suspected subversives when the García men arrived. The National Guard patrolled Rodrigo's neighborhood, sometimes stopping to rough up some of his friends. Others were simply taken away. Rodrigo avoided trouble. He had become best friends with a boy whose father was an officer in the National Police. They took their girlfriends to the movies in the officer's antique sedan and played with the black machine pistol he kept tucked away in his closet. The family owned one of the finest houses in all of Soyapango. They roasted whole calves for their parties and hired mariachi bands to entertain. Rodrigo lost many friends because he spent so much time at the house. The neighbors hated the officer and all he represented.

By the time he reached the age of seventeen, Rodrigo had learned to build houses by working with his older brothers. But they were having trouble finding jobs. As 1978 drew to a close, Rodrigo and one of his brothers vowed to get a fresh start with the new year. They would go back to Guatemala and look for work there.

He stayed with his sister, María, and her husband. They lived in a small town a few hours from Guatemala City. There, Rodrigo met a man who sold radio batteries. After Rodrigo had helped him stock shelves for a week or so, the salesman sent his young helper to the company headquarters in Guatemala City. The manager there offered Rodrigo a job. As he returned to his sister's home that night to pick up his clothes, the bus he was on broke down.

Rodrigo and two other young men decided to hitchhike. They had walked for about a half hour when they saw a pair of headlights in the distance. An onion truck, one of Rodrigo's friends said. They would surely get a ride.

But when the big truck rumbled to a halt in front of them, the three young men suddenly found themselves surrounded by soldiers. An officer ordered them to produce their papers. Because he had gone to apply for a job, Rodrigo was carrying his birth certificate. With that sort of identification, he thought, at least they would not think he was a guerrilla. They would also know he was seventeen, too young for the army. Still, Rodrigo felt himself shaking.

"Why are you trembling?" the officer asked Rodrigo. "You look like a girl." He then tore up the birth certificate and ordered Rodrigo and the others to get into the back of the truck with the other "recruits." Rodrigo had only been in Guatemala two weeks and already he was in the army, a force then conducting an even bloodier counterinsurgency campaign than the country had seen a decade earlier.

Although virtually wiped out in the late 1960s, elements of the guerrilla forces survived. After the 1976 earthquake, they resurfaced as the Guerrilla Army of the Poor (EGP). Other rebel groups also sprang up with names such as the Rebel Armed Forces (FAR) and the Revolutionary Organization of the People in Arms (ORPA). Better armed and trained than their predecessors, they made a point of recruiting and organizing among the highlands Indians, who had not been part of the earlier rebellion.

The guerrillas would arrive in a village and lecture the people on the need for armed struggle. The army would usually follow close on their heels to punish peasants it suspected of sympathizing with the call to arms. The brutality only made the peasants more receptive. An economic downturn had increased the prices they paid for food and fuel. At the same time, oil and mining companies, with army help, had begun gobbling up even more of their land.

The government was facing growing opposition from other sectors as well. Despite government harassment, the union movement continued to grow. In the late 1970s, there were major

strikes by miners, teachers, sugar workers, and government employees. The labor activity was not without government retribution. When Coca-Cola workers in Guatemala City organized to
increase their pay (then $2.50 for a twelve-hour work day), they
were beaten by military police. One by one, their leaders were
shot.

Although their numbers were also thinned by the death squads
and security forces, students and faculty at the University of
San Carlos in Guatemala City continued helping the union and
peasant groups organize. They also offered the poor free legal
help so that they could take their human rights cases to court.

The church, which had long given its blessings to the military
and the oligarchy, had become a force for change as well. Combined with the Vatican's decision to take up the cause of the poor,
an influx of foreign priests led to the growth of new religious organizations in the countryside, organizations that taught the
peasants to organize and lobby on their own behalf.

By the time Rodrigo García was impressed into the army, however, these opposition groups were being terrorized by the new
military regime of Gen. Romeo Lucas García. With the fall of the
Somoza dictatorship in Nicaragua and the increasing insurgency
in neighboring El Salvador, Lucas García came to power in 1978
vowing to wage an all-out war on the opposition. In this, he was
a success. In 1981, Amnesty International estimated that 5,000
Guatemalans had been murdered during the first three years of
Lucas García's rule. Another 615 had disappeared after being arrested by the security forces. "There are no political prisoners in
Guatemala," the country's vice-president said before going into
exile, "only political murders."

Along with their physical training, Rodrigo and the other
recruits got a strong dose of political indoctrination. The officers
told them they were to defend Guatemalan democracy. Their
enemy was the Communists, who wanted to enslave the nation.
There were subversives everywhere, in the schools, the fields, and
the factories. It was the army's duty to help root them out, but
most of all, their job was to destroy the guerrillas who hid in the

mountains.

Their drill chants reinforced what they learned in the class-room. "I am thirsty, I am thirsty," Rodrigo and the others sang as they ran. "I need the blood of the guerrilla."

Rodrigo was an intelligent, hard-working soldier. He quickly rose to the rank of corporal and his officers began telling him he might have a good future in the army. He believed it, too, and took an advanced training course that extended his thirty-month enlistment for an extra year.

But after witnessing the murder of one "subversive" at his post near the Salvadoran border, Rodrigo wondered how far a man had to go to be a good soldier. He took part in other things that bothered him. One night he was with a patrol that threw grenades into the home of an alleged subversive without knowing who else might be inside the house. Another day he was part of a unit assigned to fire mortar shells into what was supposed to be a guer-rilla stronghold. Looking toward the target area on a distant hill-side, Rodrigo could only see a small peasant village.

At the very least, Rodrigo decided he had to get away from the fighting. With a friend's help, he was transferred to a desk job at a large command center in the east. Life there was better. Rodri-go wrote training manuals and helped with special operations. Among other things, he oversaw the army's distribution of food, medicine, and building supplies in the nearby villages, a program designed to make the people believe that the military was on their side.

Within two years of entering the army, Rodrigo was promoted to the rank of first sergeant and given a job training new recruits. He was a tough and sometimes harsh drill instructor. Occasional-ly, he woke his men in the middle of the night, forced them into the showers with their uniforms on, then ordered them back to bed while they were still wet.

Rodrigo seemed to be the perfect soldier, but he knew he had begun to change. He visited his older sister, María, several times a week and told her of his desire to leave the army. She lived near the base with her husband and four daughters. María was a teacher. Like their father years before, she was also a union ac-tivist. The schoolteachers' union had always been among Guate-

mala's most militant. It had been in the forefront of the 1944 effort
to oust Ubico and, despite arrest and intimidation, it had been organizing and striking ever since.

María had gotten veiled threats from officers at Rodrigo's base.
They warned her about going out after school to conduct reading
classes in the homes of the peasants. Something might happen to
you, they said. María knew the army was watching her, which is
why she did not totally trust Rodrigo when he began asking her
to help him desert.

Still, María and her husband spent many hours talking with
Rodrigo about the army and what it was doing in Guatemala.
There was much to discuss.

In addition to the murders and disappearances in the cities,
peasants were being massacred in the rural areas. In May 1978,
several hundred Ketchi Indians gathered in the eastern town of
Panzos to protest being pushed off their land by wealthy cattle
ranchers. When they had gathered in the town square, army
troops surrounded them. After an argument between a soldier
and one of the Indians, the soldiers opened fire. Before the shooting stopped, more than one hundred Indians had died.

Just to the west, there was also trouble in Quiché Province.
Indians there had had similar problems gaining title to the lands
they had farmed for centuries. Instead of looking into their
claims, the government dispatched military police to the village
of Chajul. Peasant leaders were tortured, murdered, and disappeared. Later, the army began occupying nearby villages and air
force planes made bombing runs on what were ostensibly guerrilla stongholds, killing farm animals and destroying crops.

In November 1979, a peasant delegation went to Guatemala
City to publicize their plight, but neither the media nor the
government paid much attention. Two months later, they occupied the Spanish Embassy. Over the protests of the Spanish
ambassador, Guatemalan security forces attacked. In the scuffle,
one of the occupiers knocked over a Molotov cocktail. Thirty-four
demonstrators died in the ensuing fire, as did several embassy
employees and two visiting Guatemalan officials. The only peasant survivor was taken from his hospital bed that night and killed.

"I started to feel the pain of the others," Rodrigo says, recalling those stories. "I couldn't punish the soldiers like I once did."

He tried to hide his feelings as best he could, but Rodrigo felt the officers watching him. One day, he opened his mail to find pamphlets from several guerrilla organizations. Rodrigo knew that, even if the guerrillas wanted to contact him, they would not do so in such a brazen way. On guard duty, Rodrigo began to get calls on the base telephone. "Hey, what's your name," the caller would ask. When he told him, the caller would reply, "You're a guerrilla, aren't you?"

Rodrigo began making his plans. In the spring of 1982, he asked for a leave to go swimming at the coast with friends. When his friends returned, they told authorities Rodrigo had gotten drunk and disappeared in the surf. Rodrigo had another sister living in the base town, one who did not know of his plans. When she heard he was missing, she went to the base commander and convinced him to send a team of frogmen to look for Rodrigo's body. She also put an ad in *El Grafico*, one of Guatemala's largest newspapers, asking for information about her brother.

Rodrigo read the ad from his hiding place in Guatemala City. He stayed with friends for two months, then took a bus to the Mexican border. His friends drove ahead of his bus, watching for army roadblocks. Rodrigo convinced Mexican immigration officials to give him a three-day visitor's pass. From there he went to Tapachula, the largest Mexican city near the border.

The Guatemalan army had not forgotten him, nor did his commanders believe he had drowned. Troops raided María's house three times looking for Rodrigo and police kept a close watch on their father's home in Guatemala City. Soon after Rodrigo's departure, one of his brothers — also a union leader — disappeared. A few months later, his father was arrested at his office one morning.

María's two oldest daughters, ages nine and ten, were visiting their grandfather at the time. On the day Arturo was arrested, María was coming in from the countryside to pick up the girls. The family planned to have a party that night. She walked down her father's block that afternoon to see his house surrounded by police cars and soldiers. María asked one of the soldiers what had happened. When she told him it was her father's home, he grabbed her by the arm, but she pulled away and ran.

That night, María sat at a relative's house, weeping and waiting for news. The next morning, the newspapers were full of it.
The army reported that it had uncovered a guerrilla arsenal at the
home of seventy-year-old Arturo García. In addition to María's
father and several other relatives, they had also taken away her
two daughters.

María spent the next two years roaming Guatemala City's
orphanages and hospitals in search of her daughters. She never
saw them or her father again. Unable to return to her home, she
too finally fled to Mexico.

In six months, Rodrigo had gone from a soldier in command
of many lives to a refugee who was powerless to control his own.
There were thousands of displaced Guatemalans and Salvadorans
drifting through the streets of Tapachula. For a time, Rodrigo
knocked on doors and begged for food. Eventually, he went to a
church for help. The priest told Rodrigo he could stay in the rear
courtyard with the other refugees.

Two other refugee families were living there when Rodrigo arrived. They included Lucas Martínez and his family. Rodrigo fell
in love with the elderly Salvadoran's daughter, Vicky. Eventually,
they married, but it was a difficult time for love to bloom. The
growing community of refugees slept on strips of cardboard and
in hammocks. Some used sticks and coconut leaves to build small
huts. Others slept under thin plastic tarps. They depended on the
church for everything.

Rodrigo did not want to live this way. Although he risked
arrest and deportation by the Mexican authorities, the former
soldier began leaving the compound to paint houses and do what
odd jobs he could find. He helped other churches build homes for
the refugees coming to their doors.

The refugee work began taking up more and more of his time.
He delivered medicine and supplies to the camps in the countryside and led journalists, church groups, and international human
rights investigators on tours of the area.

Rodrigo was sitting in the churchyard one day when a tall, thin

gringo came through the gates. He had a moustache and glasses
and always seemed to be smiling. The man told Rodrigo he represented a group of North American church people who were
helping Central Americans.

"He began talking wildly about what he could offer the refugees
in the United States," Rodrigo recalled. "I did not trust him at
first. I said, 'What kind of person is that who is talking like this
so publicly and so dangerously?' "

5

From Declaration
to Movement

Rodrigo García was not the first person to be unnerved by Jim Corbett's zeal. In southern Mexico, cautious people did not speak openly about aiding the Central Americans. Those who did risked reprisal from the Mexican government and perhaps even the Guatemalan Army.

By the time Corbett endured his first long and bumpy bus ride from Tucson to Tapachula, Chiapas, in November 1981, thousands of Central Americans had sought refuge in southern Mexico. The more urbanized Salvadorans tended to stop briefly before moving on to Mexico City or the United States. Most refugees who remained were peasants from the nearby Guatemalan highlands; many were Indians with the same Mayan heritage as those who made up roughly 40 percent of the population of Chiapas.

Some of the refugees had aided the guerrillas who roamed the Guatemalan mountains. Most had not. Fate had simply placed their villages and small farms in the path of the Guatemalan Army's scorched-earth war against the rebels. Five hundred refugees came to Los Lagos de Montebellos in January 1981. That same month, thirteen hundred filtered into Paso Hondo. By mid-1982, there were an estimated twenty thousand refugees living in the camps and jungles of Chiapas. Few spoke Spanish. The majority were less than twenty years old, and roughly 20 percent of them were four years old or less. In addition to psychological trauma, many arrived suffering from malnutrition, parasites, and malaria.

The Catholic dioceses of San Cristóbal and Tapachula provided them with what food, medicine, and building materials they could muster, but the church aid was not enough.

The Mexican government, which recognized only those refugees who had settled into the camps, responded with a tangled and unpredictable mixture of aid and animosity. In July 1980, it established the Mexican Commission to Aid the Refugees (COMAR) to coordinate relief efforts, but its allocation and delivery of supplies was spotty and inadequte. Moreover, COMAR never seemed to speak for the entire Mexican government. In 1981, even as the COMAR director was announcing that there would be no mass deportations, Mexican immigration agents in Chiapas were pushing two thousand refugees back across the border at gunpoint. Local authorities denounced church officials, Mexican Indian leaders, and even doctors who helped the refugees.

It was an ironic response for a country that had a long history of offering asylum to political refugees. In 1937, Leon Trotsky had been welcomed after Joseph Stalin muscled his way to power in Moscow. More recently, refuge had been granted to Argentines, Chileans, and Uruguayans running from military repression in their countries.

Mexico had also been outspoken in its calls for reform in Central America. The government supported the Sandinista revolution in Nicaragua and severed diplomatic relations with dictator Anastasio Somoza in the final months of his regime. Mexico had also offered moral and diplomatic support to guerrillas fighting to overthrow the government of El Salvador.

But tradition and speeches were forgotten when it came to Guatemala and the situation in Chiapas, one of Mexico's poorest states. The land was fertile enough to support dozens of coffee, sugar, and banana plantations. The state was also rich in oil, timber, and grazing land. But, as in Guatemala, a small moneyed elite controlled much of the land. They maintained their position with corruption, political pull, and sheer force.

The peasants were left to scrape out a living on the meager plots that remained and, along with thousands of their Guatemalan brothers and sisters, to provide cheap labor for the plantations. For the Indians, life was a dark cycle of poverty and exploitation. Their rates of unemployment, illiteracy, and infant mortality were among the highest in Mexico. They had occasionally rebelled, especially when the wealthy seized communal land. But with the Mexican army in its corner, the ruling elite never had problems smothering the uprisings. Still, Indian unrest remained among its worst fears. The fact that leftists were organizing peasants in the nearby Guatemalan highlands did nothing to calm their nerves. The possibility that some of those politicized Guatemalans might mix with their own Indians sent shudders through the ranks of the rich.

The refugees' presence had also become a point of contention with Guatemala, Mexico's well-armed neighbor to the south. Relations between the two countries had rarely risen above mutual suspicion. The right-wing generals who ran Guatemala resented being overshadowed by their larger, more influential neighbor. They had not forgotten the nineteenth-century loss of Chiapas to Mexico nor that Mexico had supported independence for Belize, the former British colony that Guatemala still claimed as its own.

The Guatemala military was certainly in no mood for brotherhood with a country offering moral support to Central American leftists. To the Guatemalan military, these priests, teachers, journalists, and peasant leaders were Communists and they knew how to deal with them. In the cities, subversives real and imagined were hunted down by police and paramilitary death squads. In the provinces, villages were leveled as the army moved to depopulate vast stretches of land in order to deny the guerrillas their base of support. The survivors were moved into "model villages" built and controlled by the military.

In a February 1981 report, Amnesty International called the campaign a "government program for political murder." In reply, Gen. Romeo Lucas García, the Guatemalan president, dubbed the international human rights group "an agency of the red dictatorships" and vowed that his government "would resort to all the extremes that the law establishes to prevent the traitors from trying to seize power."

As Mexico soon discovered, that extremism extended beyond Guatemala's borders. In June 1981, Guatemalan troops began taking their hunt for subversives into Mexico, ostensibly to seize guerrillas hiding among the refugees. Later, helicopter gunships joined the hunt. Mexican farmers were sometimes caught in the crossfire. For Mexico, the incursions involved an attack on its territorial integrity. The government was also worried that the presence of the refugees might lead to military conflict with Guatemala and endanger the rich oil fields near its 565-mile southern border.

Into this tension strolled a tall and talkative gringo offering smuggling services that could only draw more refugees into Chiapas. Clearly, Jim Corbett was not the sort of tourist Mexico wanted wandering around its southern border. But the Arizona Quaker, already defying the dictates and policies of his own government, was not deterred. He saw the governments of Mexico and the United States as coconspirators in a plot to deny the Central Americans their international rights as refugees. "Mexico has obviously agreed to protect the U.S. borders from refugees," he wrote to a friend a few months before his first Chiapas visit. "Information about ways to evade the Mexican migra [immigration authorities] would do more than anything else right now to reduce losses."

While in Chiapas, Corbett planned to scout immigration roadblocks and border surveillance as a prelude to bringing refugees up through Mexico. He also wanted to establish some sort of sanctuary outpost along the Guatemala border. After six months of smuggling refugees in Arizona, Corbett had concluded that most needed help long before they reached northern Mexico and southern Arizona. Too many were being beaten, raped, and robbed in Mexico, by both coyotes and police. And too many were getting caught and deported by the U.S. Immigration and Naturalization Service because they didn't know what to do when they reached the United States.

Corbett wanted to spread the word about himself and Southside Presbyterian through priests and refugee workers in southern Mexico and eventually in Central America itself. In addition to providing the refugees with practical information about the best way to travel north, Corbett hoped to find sympathizers along the Guatemalan border who would notify him of particularly desperate cases. One of the North American sanctuary workers would then go to southern Mexico to escort the refugee to the U.S. border.

But in late 1981, that was no more than a plan in Corbett's head. He did not know the roads, rivers, and jungles of southern Mexico, nor was he certain of the best way to slip a refugee past the Mexican authorities. For that matter, Corbett had no idea who in Chiapas would help him. All he had to go on were the stories the refugees in Arizona had told him. "Playing it by ear," he called it.

After a stop to visit Quakers in Mexico City, Corbett arrived in Tapachula on November 21. The railroad yards were full of Guatemalan men looking for a place to go. Many of the women were even less fortunate. They ended up trying to earn bus fare in the city's brothels.

Over the next few days, Corbett took several short bus trips out into the countryside. He went south to the coastal village of Puerto Madero and north to the coffee-growing area of Caca-hoatán. At the small border village at Ciudad Hidalgo, he watched as Guatemalan women with loads on their heads waded the Suchiate River undisturbed by Mexican immigration officers on a nearby bridge. Upstream, people crossed the river on truck inner tubes. The authorities only stopped those who looked as though they were not from the area. Salvadorans were easy targets to spot. They wore different clothes than the Guate-malans. Along the riverbank, a woman pointed to a shoe and told Corbett it had obviously come from a dead Salvadoran who had been pulled from the river a few days earlier.

In the villages, Corbett spoke with people on the streets, pre-tending to be a tourist with nothing better to do. He got them talking about the situation on the border by asking whether they thought it would be a good time for him to tour Guatemala. One peasant asked Corbett if he was a Guatemalan, explaining that he looked very much like someone from that country who was hiding out in the village.

Some of the poor Mexicans in the area were already sharing their land with Guatemalans, but most had little to offer other than a place to put up a shanty. Even such meager charity was not universal. In the Tapacula newspaper, Corbett read of state

officials who blamed the Central Americans for rises in the rates
of unemployment and street crime. He talked openly about his
mission with the priests he met, but many of them were less than
anxious to help. One priest told him he was too busy with his
church duties to know whether there were any refugees running
around. Besides, the clergyman added, they were a dirty, un-
couth lot who didn't fit into the local culture.

From the stories he had heard in Arizona, Corbett was able to
find one area priest who was, in essence, operating a one-man
sanctuary movement along the border. The priest had been running the refugees past the immigration checkpoints, giving them
food and housing, and finding them jobs. He invited Corbett to
tell of his work in Arizona at a church retreat. There he found
dozens more Mexicans willing to help the cause. Corbett ce-
mented the relationship by giving the priest $420 toward his work
with the refugees.

The situation in Guatemala was less promising. After he
crossed the border on December 4, Corbett wrote to his wife, Pat,
to tell her what he found:

Dec. 4: Nothing can be done, organizationally, to
try to help the deportees. The few priests left are the
only ones who could be contacts, but they wouldn't last
long if outsiders were in touch with them. A little
money so they can offer something to the destitute —
that's about it.

Dec. 5: A few moments ago, I was in the plaza,
sitting and watching the evening promenade, when
there was a burst of pistol fire from the police station
about 50 yards from me. Everyone scurried for cover,
and businesses quickly shut their doors and turned off
their inside lights. I walked over to a place where a bus
driver and passengers were peering from the corner of
a building. There were lots of ideas about a guerrilla
attack, but no one really knew why the police started
shooting.

The daily paper has six stories about 11 disappearances and three stories about seven recovered corpses,
all written in ways that indicate the death squad got

them. . . . Many of these stories are tucked away among ads in back pages, like fillers. The death squads are clearly working all over, not just in insurgent strongholds, reports of disappearances being from every part of the country.

Corbett returned to Tucson a week before Christmas. He immediately began pounding out more letters to his friends and planning for his next trip to Chiapas. In the months that followed, the arthritic Arizonan blazed trails through the Chiapan jungle and made contact with priests and nuns inside Guatemala and El Salvador. He learned that by dressing Salvadorans as Guatemalans, he could get them past Mexican authorities along the river. He found the back roads where there were no checkpoints.

The work was dangerous and eventually a friendly Mexican priest warned Corbett that there was a price on his head. Still he returned and other North Americans came with him. By car, bus, train, and plane, they brought dozens of refugees to Mexico City and Hermosillo, then on to the United States.

Meanwhile, thousands more refugees continued to come to Chiapas. By the end of 1982, COMAR estimated that there were thirty-six thousand refugees living in rough, makeshift camps along the border. Church-aid groups believed as many as one hundred thousand more had moved farther into Mexico. Refugee workers from the United Nations moved in to help coordinate relief efforts, but at times it was impossible to get medicine and supplies to those living deep in the jungle. Disease and malnutrition were rampant, especially among the children.

"There is no infrastructure of health care here," a doctor at one camp near Puerto Rico told reporter Juan Vásquez of the *Los Angeles Times*. "We can dispense medicine and maybe that will stop the aching and the diarrhea for a day or two. But without food and clean water and permanent health care, they will just get sick again."

Disease and hunger were not the refugees' only enemies. Although the Mexican government had stopped the deportations, Guatemalan troops continued trying to repatriate the refugees forcibly. In September 1982, they raided the village of Castillo Tielemans and beat several Mexicans before returning to their country with seven to ten refugees. Three weeks later, they attacked the El Recuerdo refugee camp. Two refugees were killed in November when one hundred Guatemalan soldiers descended on the Santiago el Vértice camp.

Meanwhile, in Washington the Reagan administration was making plans to resume military aid to Guatemala. Jimmy Carter had suspended military shipments to Guatemala in 1977 because of human rights abuses there. But on a visit to Honduras in December 1982, Ronald Reagan had met with Efraín Ríos Montt, the latest general to seize control of the Guatemalan government. The American president had come away impressed with the general's commitment to democracy.

By the middle of 1982, sanctuary had begun to expand beyond the confines of southern Arizona and the San Francisco Bay area. It put down roots in the nation's heartland on July 18, 1982, when the Wellington Avenue United Church of Christ in Chicago — with the support of dozens of other area churches — voted to declare itself a sanctuary. Pastor David Chevrier announced the decision in a letter to U.S. Attorney General William French Smith.

"This action," he wrote, "which we take after months of prayer and deliberation, reflects our belief that the current policy and practice of the United States Government with regard to Central American refugees is illegal and immoral. . . . We ask you to do all within your power to bring justice to these desperate people. Grant these refugees Extended Voluntary Departure status and stop the current atrocious deportation proceedings that return these people to death and government retribution."

Wellington Avenue was a small Northside church with a diverse congregation and a long history of political activism. It housed demonstrators during the 1968 Democratic Convention. In the years that followed, church members began working at the precinct level to defeat Chicago Mayor Richard Daley's political machine. In 1974, Wellington Avenue decided to let a gay congregation use its building for evening services. During the seventies, church members also launched letter-writing campaigns on behalf of political prisoners in South Africa, South Korea, Chile, and other countries.

Central American refugees became an issue at Wellington Avenue after a member of the congregation, the Rev. Sid Mohn, went to El Salvador in January 1982 at the request of the National Council of Churches. The council began sending North American ministers to El Salvador after hearing reports that security forces there were terrorizing refugee camps. Socorro Jurídico, the legal aid office of the archdiocese of El Salvador, had documented more than sixty such attacks between August 1980 and March 1981. They included instances of robberies, beatings, murders, and detentions. The council hoped the ministers could provide some protection with their presence.

After he returned to Chicago, Mohn conducted a special service on the refugees' plight. With his stories still fresh in the minds of the congregation, church leaders sent a letter of support to Southside Presbyterian Church in Tucson after they read news accounts of its sanctuary declaration.

A few weeks later, a representative of the Chicago Religious Task Force on Central America (CRTFCA) asked the church council whether Wellington Avenue would consider making a declaration in support of sanctuary for the Central America refugees.

The request was an outgrowth of the Tucson group's campaign to recruit sanctuary churches and supporters outside the border region. One reason for Tucson's outreach was political: changing the Reagan administration's deportation policy would require more grass-roots political pressure than could be mustered in sparsely populated southern Arizona. The other reason was practical: Southside Presbyterian's March 24 declaration had attracted more attention than the Tucson volunteers could handle. "The phone was going off the wall day and night with refugees getting in touch with us," says John Fife. "We discovered refugees we didn't even know existed in Tucson, let alone all along the border. We were also getting letters and calls from churches wanting to know more, and from reporters and journalists saying 'Can you take us on a trip to the border?' Suddenly, we were inundated with things to do."

The Arizona sanctuary organizers decided that if they were to continue concentrating on direct aid to refugees on the border, they would have to find other groups farther from the crisis zone who could organize and coordinate the movement. Corbett and others began giving talks to church groups around the country and sending letters to potential supporters. "The Tucson refugee support groups urgently need to make contact with religious fellowships of all denominations throughout the U.S. that will declare public sanctuary for undocumented refugees," Corbett wrote in one plea. "Overnight shelter and city-to-city transportation for cross-country relays are most needed. We are asking no one to divert money or energy from worthy causes. Just make your place of worship available as a temporary refuge for fugitive Salvadorans and Guatemalans who will occasionally pass through. And tell both the public and those who would prohibit such aid exactly where you stand."

CRTFCA was one of the organizations contacted. The task force, founded one month after the December 1980 murder of four North American churchwomen in El Salvador, was an interdenominational group dedicated to turning public opinion against U.S. policy in Central America. "Our task," said a later CRTFCA publication, "is to inform, educate and activate people on the conditions in Central America, to expose the role of the U.S. government in maintaining corrupt and repressive governments in that area and in promoting policies designed to destabilize the government of Nicaragua."

Through 1981 and 1982, CRTFCA members talked to area church groups, organized Central American cultural programs, and tried to pressure Illinois Senator Charles Percy, then chairman of the Senate Foreign Relations Committee, into opposing the Reagan policy. Aside from the occasional demonstration, they got little notice. But the task force was among the few organizations the Tucson group could find that were organized around the Central American issue.

Although the task force contacted Wellington Avenue Church in response to Tucson's call for help, its members were not anxious to take on the organization of a nationwide movement. They had few volunteers, very little money, and almost no contacts outside the Chicago area. Corbett was still trying to persuade them to accept the job even as Wellington Avenue was moving toward a declaration of sanctuary.

With little debate, the Wellington Avenue Church Council voted to support the idea of sanctuary. A few weeks later, the CRTFCA representative returned and asked the church to open its doors to the refugees. Unwilling to make that decision on its own, the council decided to put the idea to a vote of the congregation. After a committee of church members investigated the legal, financial, and theological implications of such a move, the idea was put before the congregation after services on Sunday, July 11.

A few worried that the small church could not sustain the financial burden of supporting a family of refugees. Beyond the money, no one could tell them for certain how the federal government would react. Would federal marshals appear at the church some Sunday and arrest them all? Most members of the congregation agreed that they should do something to help the Salvadorans and Guatemalans, but many questioned the wisdom of doing so publicly. Why dare the federal government to move against them?

The vote was scheduled for the following Sunday. In the area to speak at nearby Notre Dame University, John Fife came to the church that day along with a young Salvadoran woman named Alicia. Before the congregation made its decision, she told them about her life as a catechist in San Salvador. The security forces had shot her priest and tortured one of her fellow church workers. Such things were not unusual, she told them. The vultures in El Salvador were well fed. People had even gotten used to seeing dogs running down the street with human feet and hands in their mouths. Alicia and her teenaged brother and sister had fled after the security forces came looking for her.

"It became clear why it had to become public," says Chevrier. "The issue was not just protecting lives that were in danger in Chicago and the United States. The lives that were in danger were in El Salvador. If we were to stop that, the American people had to be informed on what was going on there."

By a vote of fifty-nine to four, the congregation decided to be-

come a sanctuary. Six days later, Wellington Avenue opened it
chapel to a twenty-seven-year-old Salvadoran student. A week
later, Corbett escorted a Salvadoran family to Chicago in one of
the first cross-country relays of the movement's underground
railroad.

While in Chicago, Corbett made one more attempt to persuade
the task force to coordinate the movement. This time, it agreed.
In addition to publishing a manual on how to declare sanctuary,
the task force sent organizers to Milwaukee and Washington to
speak with congregations then debating the issue.

On December 2, the second anniversary of the murder of
North American churchwomen in El Salvador, Archbishop
Rembert Weakland of Milwaukee opened parishes there to the
refugees. That same day, the University Baptist Church in
Seattle, Washington, also declared sanctuary. Ten days later,
St. Luke's Presbyterian Church outside Minneapolis made its
announcement.

The activity attracted the attention of the *Chicago Tribune,* the
Christian Science Monitor, Newsweek, the *London Times,* and the
Washington Post as well as dozens of smaller papers. In August,
People magazine published an account of Jim Corbett smuggling
one family up from Mexico. The CBS program "60 Minutes" sent
correspondent Ed Bradley to Tucson. The resulting story, broad-
cast in December 1982, featured footage of Corbett bringing a
Salvadoran family across the border.

In Washington, the Immigration and Naturalization Service
had begun fielding dozens of calls from reporters who wanted to
know what the INS was planning to do about the sanctuary movement. INS spokesman Duke Austin's response to an Associated
Press reporter was typical: "It's always been the policy of the INS
that we do not conduct area control operations—sweeps or raids
—in neighborhoods, residences or churches."

But the government was taking no chances. Following the publication of the *People* article, INS officials and investigators met in
Phoenix to discuss the growing movement. They decided to forward what material they had to the Justice Department for
review.

In December 1982, Renny Golden, a member of the Chicago

Religious Task Force on Central America, published articles on sanctuary in two religious magazines, *Sojourners* and *The Witness*. In a memo distributed to INS officials in Arizona, California, and Washington, D.C., an INS intelligence agent in Yuma, Arizona, wrote that "at this point, it appears that some churches are using the sanctuary concept to rally congregations, and create cohesiveness in Hispanic parishes. This type of movement is particularly attractive to pastors with a political bent that are seeking a cause. Those who are normally satisfied to vent their ill humors in *Sojourners* would consider sanctuary as de rigor [*sic*]. Risks would be minimal, considering the reluctance of the state to incur the wrath of the church. Whatever liability that is incurred from sanctuary can be written off by the relative merits of gaining martyrdom."

Meanwhile, the deportations continued. During fiscal year 1983, the INS granted political asylum to 163 Salvadorans. It denied it to forty times that many.

6

The Reagan Response

At times, the Reagan administration responded to the growing movement like an exasperated father who wasn't quite sure what to do with his errant child. With each new sanctuary declaration, an official from the State Department or the INS would step forward to assert that the refugees were coming to the United States for economic reasons. This country has asylum laws to protect those who could prove they faced persecution back home, they would say. It was a pity the pastors and housewives in the sanctuary movement could not understand that.

"We're concerned that they don't want to take the legal avenues available to them," said INS commissioner Alan C. Nelson. "As far as we're concerned, there is no basis in current U.S. law for sanctuary." Nevertheless, he added that there were no plans to send INS agents crashing into the churches to arrest the refugees or their hosts. "We feel that the smugglers—those people who are doing it for profit—those are the people we are concentrating on. You have to have priorities."

Some immigration authorities were less reserved. In a December 1982 interview with the *Arizona Daily Star,* Tucson Border Patrol Chief Leon Ring said he "put alien smuggling in the same category as slave trading." But for the most part, administration officials took pains not to be too impolite when criticizing the sanctuary churches. They usually made certain to imply, however, that the movement was up to something less than humanitarian. In an interview with the PBS program "Frontline," Nelson allowed that the sanctuary people were "well meaning,"

but "Many of them will admit what they are really doing is opposing the president's policy in Central America." The implica-
tion was that the sanctuary leaders were hiding cynical political
goals behind all the Good Samaritan talk.

The religious and humanitarian motivations of the movement
did tend to get the most attention. This was probably inevitable,
since most of its leaders were active church members and most of
the refugees they introduced to the press had heartbreaking
stories to tell. But the political goals of sanctuary were never clandestine. The movement was not smuggling refugees merely to
satisfy religious commandments or provide the press with a few
good headlines. It wanted the deportation of Salvadorans and
Guatemalans stopped. Since immigration policy is seldom set by
theologians or sociologists, the sanctuary movement had to argue
with politicians.

Beyond the deportation issue, the movement hoped to persuade Americans to reconsider their government's support of
regimes the refugees were fleeing. This too was political. It was
also a logical extension of the sanctuary movement's work. By
aiding refugees in the United States, the movement was dealing
with the results of the human rights atrocities in Central America.
By applying political and economic pressure to the military
governments of the region, via their benefactors in Washington,
it was attacking the source.

American churches have a long tradition of political involvement, and civil disobedience has often played a part. In the
1850s, New England churches defied the fugitive slave laws by
running the underground railroad. A century later, a Baptist
preacher named Martin Luther King Jr., launched the modern
civil rights movement to protest the segregation laws of the South.
Ten years after that, American ministers were in the forefront of
the antiwar movement.

"Almost every moral issue is political and every political issue
is moral," said the Rev. Dick Sinner, a Tucson priest active in the
sanctuary movement. "To make a judgement that you don't get
involved in these issues is to avoid a very important element in
our ministry. . . . This is no different from what the German
people had to do when they smuggled their Jewish friends out of

the country into Italy and into Holland, Denmark and Norway
to avoid the Nazi oppression."

The movement might have avoided trouble with Washington
by continuing to smuggle and shelter the refugees far from the
eyes of public and press. Remaining underground would have
made life easier for them and the few hundred refugees they
helped. It would have done nothing for the tens of thousands
coming on their own or the hundreds of thousands still in the
Mexican jungles and in refugee camps within their countries. By
early 1983, the fighting had forced an estimated 250,000 Salvadorans to leave the rural areas and move to the refugee camps and
slums of the cities. At least that many had left the country and
gone to the United States. Another 50,000 were refugees in other
Central American countries. In Guatemala, the violence had left
100,000 people homeless. Another 25,000 or more were refugees
in Mexico.

"We decided to go public because we'd all become aware that
a full-scale holocaust was going on in Central America," said
John Fife. "By keeping the operation clandestine, we were doing
exactly what the government wanted us to do — keeping it hidden,
keeping the issue out of public view."

By working in the open, however, they also became players in
a game of hardball politics with the conservative Reagan administration. Although small, the sanctuary movement was an affront
to the very foundation of the Reagan vision. The churches did not
possess the money or influence to present a serious political challenge to the popular president, but New Right preachers such as
the Rev. Jerry Falwell had shown the Reagan team that the pulpit
could be a pivotal force in plotting the nation's political agenda.
With the voices of the refugees it smuggled into the country, the
movement was attempting to set an agenda that strayed far from
the Reagan doctrines on immigration, human rights, and — most
important to the president — the threat of communism in the
Western Hemisphere. It was around this last point that the
conflict between church and state ultimately revolved.

Reagan, along with first-term advisers such as Secretary of
State Alexander Haig and U.N. Ambassador Jeane Kirkpatrick,
saw the Soviet hammer and sickle lurking behind every revolu-

tionary movement in Central America. For them, there was little difference between Hungary and Poland after World War II and El Salvador and Guatemala in the 1980s. They were all manifestations of the Kremlin's ambition for world domination. The administration set out to paint the rebels of El Salvador and Guatemala as nothing more than agents of Soviet subversion in the Western Hemisphere.

Under this same reasoning, the military governments of those two countries were pictured as the beleaguered torchbearers of democracy. The Reagan admistration argued that, although the anti-Communist leaders in Central America might not rate among the world's great humanitarians, failure to support them would pave the way for a string of Soviet puppets that stretched from the Panama Canal to the Rio Grande. "The situation is, you might say, our front yard, it isn't just El Salvador," the president told CBS News's Walter Cronkite. "What we're doing is . . . trying to halt the infiltration into the Americas by terrorists, by outside interference and those who aren't just aiming at El Salvador but, I think, are aiming at the whole of Central America and possibly later South America—and I'm sure eventually North America."

The president feared this plot so profoundly that he made proving its existence his administration's first major foreign policy initiative. One month after Reagan took office, Secretary of State Haig told NATO members of a "well-orchestrated international Communist campaign" to aid the Salvadoran rebels. "With Cuban coordination," he reported, "the Soviet bloc, Vietnam, Ethiopa and radical Arabs are furnishing at least several hundred tons of military equipment to the Salvadoran insurgents."

The following week, the State Department released a "white paper" on El Salvador. Based on intelligence reports and what were described as captured guerrilla documents, the report purported to offer "incontrovertible" proof that various Communist nations had delivered two hundred tons of military supplies to the Salvadoran rebels through Cuba and Nicaragua. "The insurgency in El Salvador has been progressively transformed to a textbook case of indirect armed aggression by Communist powers through Cuba," the white paper concluded.

Subsequent investigations by *The Nation,* the *Wall Street Journal,* and the *Washington Post* indicated that the evidence offered by the State Department did not support the conclusions reached in the report. The authorship of the rebel documents was also questioned. "The State department's white paper on El Salvador . . . contains factual errors, misleading statements and unsolved ambiguities that raise questions about the administration's interpretation of participation by communist countries in the Salvadoran civil war," the *Washington Post* reported.

But the administration stuck to its guns. A week after the white paper's release, Reagan sent twenty more U.S. military advisers to El Salvador along with $25 million in additional military aid. Congress subsequently passed a law making all future military aid contingent on a certification by the president that the Salvadoran government was making progress on human rights. Drawing its figures from Salvadoran press reports, the U.S. Embassy in San Salvador reported 5,407 political killings in 1981. The legal office of the Salvadoran archdiocese put the figure at 13,353. Nevertheless, one month in 1982, the administration told Congress the Salvadoran government's improving human rights record merited continued military aid.

At the same time, the Reagan administration was moving to reopen the supply lines to Gen. Romeo Lucas García in Guatemala. U.S. military aid to Guatemala had been suspended since 1977, when the Carter administration had issued a report critical of human rights abuses by the Guatemalan government. One month after Reagan took office, Amnesty International reported that nearly five thousand Guatemalans had been killed since Lucas García became president in 1978. "The bodies of the victims have been found piled up in ravines, dumped at the roadsides or buried in mass graves," the report said. "Thousands bore the scars of torture, and death had come to most by strangling with a garrote, by being suffocated in rubber hoods or by being shot in the head."

Despite such accounts, in June 1981 the Reagan administration approved the sale of $3.2 million worth of jeeps and trucks to the Lucas García regime. Stephen Bosworth, assistant secretary of state for inter-American affairs, explained the new approach to members of the House Commitee on Foreign Affairs the following month. The administration's objective, Bosworth testified, was to "develop a relationship with the government of Guatemala which both enhances its ability to control insurgency, guarantees the country's stability, and . . . enhances its ability to improve . . . the human rights situation in that country."

Bosworth hoped that muting public criticism of Guatemala and providing limited military aid would give the United States more leverage in influencing the country's abysmal human rights record. When asked, however, whether the delivery of the equipment a month earlier had had any such impact, Bosworth admitted it had not.

It should have been no surprise that, under Ronald Reagan, human rights took a back seat to his crusade against communism. The administration's priorities had been outlined in 1979 in a *Commentary* magazine article entitled "Dictatorships and Double Standards." In the article, Georgetown University political science professor Jeane Kirkpatrick criticized the Carter administration for failing to support pro-American "autocrats" such as Anastasio Somoza in Nicaragua and the shah in Iran. Unsavory as such despots might be, she wrote, they were reliable anti-Communists. The United States should concentrate on skewering the Eastern bloc for its abuses and use milder forms of persuasion for its allies. Ronald Reagan was so moved by Professor Kirkpatrick's reasoning that he made her his ambassador to the United Nations.

"Speaking generally, we must make it perfectly clear that we are revolted by torture and can never feel spiritual kinship with a government that engages in torture," she told *U.S. News and World Report* after her appointment. "But the central goal of our foreign policy should not be the moral elevation of other nations, but the preservation of a civilized conception of our own self-interest."

To shepherd this human rights policy of divine self-interest, Reagan chose Elliot Abrams. A former Democrat, the Harvard-educated lawyer had served on the Senate staffs of both Henry Jackson and Daniel Moynihan before joining the Reagan campaign in 1980. He spoke on the Republicans' behalf to Jewish groups around the country. He was rewarded for his work with an appointment as assistant secretary of state for human rights and humanitarian affairs.

From the start, Abrams spoke as bluntly as any human rights advocate from the Carter years, but his sights were aimed at totally different targets. "I just can't abide the fact that the left sits on its high horse and think they have a superior position on human rights because they are on the left," he told the *New York Times*. Public criticism of abuses by right-wing governments and U.S. allies was muted, when it came at all. "We think people who are friends of the United States get some points for that," Abrams said.

Although Abrams would later criticize the sanctuary movement for mixing politics with humanitarian pursuits, he articulated a policy in which the two were inextricably linked. In a Miami speech delivered less than three months after the first sanctuary declarations, Abrams said that, although the administration would continue trying to improve respect for human rights around the world, different situations would call for different tactics. "Our tactics will vary depending on our relationship with the country in question: whether it is a friend or a foe."

The foe Abrams worried about most was the Soviet Union. "We want to be very sure that in a situation such as that in El Salvador, we do not trade the serious but solvable rights problems of today for a permanent Communist dictatorship," he said at the Miami speech in June 1982. "Resisting the expansion of communism is a key human rights goal. . . . I am always amazed," he added, "when people come to me to voice their concern about refugees from El Salvador, yet who oppose the Administration's effort to avoid enlargement of that refugee problem by giving the aid it needs to defeat Communist-led guerrillas."

In the face of this spirited revival of Cold War rhetoric, sanctuary leaders were smuggling in refugees who went before microphones and offered a different perspective on the discontent in their homelands. They spoke of immense poverty and hunger, of wealthy landowners who kept them in virtual economic slavery. They also recounted in gruesome detail acts of murder, torture, and political repression by their governments. The refugees' testimony clouded the picture that the administration sought to paint of Central America as a clear-cut struggle between communism and democracy.

There was no doubt that the guerrillas in the hills of El Salvador and Guatemala were carrying Soviet weapons, but if the refugees' stories were any measure, they weren't doing so merely because they had read a few books by Karl Marx or Mao Tse-tung.

The administration could not have have spurned the refugees and their North American advocates without the support, or at least the indifference, of the public. A 1983 *New York Times*–CBS poll indicated that only about 25 percent of those questioned were aware that the United States was supporting the government of El Salvador. Coupled with the public's ignorance of the bloody situation in Central America was a growing feeling that the United States needed to curb the number of aliens it admitted. Sixty-five percent of all Americans believed their country should allow less immigration, according to a 1981 Associated Press–NBC poll.

Decades earlier, the Statue of Liberty had been a symbol of promise and shelter for millions of Germans, Irish, Italians, and Slavs sailing into New York Harbor. They came from the Old World fleeing poverty and persecution. The statue continued to proclaim our shores to be a haven for "huddled masses yearning to breathe free," but with each passing generation, the descendants of those earlier refugees had become less and less willing to share that sweet, free air with all comers.

The first serious efforts to restrict immigration began in the late nineteenth century, when Congress barred prostitutes, convicts, and mental patients from entry. As the years passed, the immigration laws began to focus more on race, politics, and economics. The Chinese Exclusion Act of 1882, for instance, was designed to protect the United States from the so-called yellow peril. Immigration from Asia and the Pacific would be heavily restricted for the next eighty years. A subsequent law permitted contract workers to enter the United States but limited their stay to one year. This kept them from putting down roots here while providing U.S. employers with a steady stream of cheap labor.

In 1921, responding to a growing number of immigrants from southern and western Europe, Congress enacted a system of immigration quotas. The numbers were skewed in favor of immigrants from northern and western Europe. Great Britain was granted forty-three percent of the total. While the quotas were supposedly designed to "preserve the national character of the United States," they were also used to deport labor organizers in the 1930s when industrialists in the northeast found their workers getting a bit too independent.

Latin America did not figure prominently in the early immigration debate. Fruit and vegetable growers in the Southwest depended on cheap Mexican labor to harvest their crops. Between 1910 and 1930, recruitment by the U.S. growers coupled with revolution in Mexico led an estimated four hundred thousand Mexicans to move north. With the Depression, fieldwork became harder to find and the newly created Border Patrol made crossing the border an even less attractive proposition for the average Mexican. Still, when the onslaught of World War II created labor shortages in the Southwest, Congress created the *bracero* program, which permitted Mexicans to work in the American fields and farmers and ranchers to get their crops harvested for substandard wages.

When the Cold War spawned a new wave of xenophobia, the Border Patrol gave national security as the reason for rounding up and deporting an estimated one million undocumented immigrants from Mexico in what was dubbed "Operation Wetback." During the McCarthy era, the federal government also employed the immigration laws to exclude those who were deemed politically undesirable.

With a few exceptions, refugees had no special status under U.S. law until World War II left millions of Europeans homeless. In 1948, Congress passed the Displaced Persons Act, which permitted the admission of up to four hundred thousand European refugees into the United States. Those admitted had to be able to prove they would not become wards of the state. Such assurances usually came in the form of sponsorship by a church or private agency.

The Immigration and Nationality Act of 1952 went a few steps farther. It authorized the attorney general to withhold deportation of aliens who faced persecution in their own countries. It also permitted the attorney general to "parole" an alien into the United States in emergency situations. After the 1956 Hungarian uprising, President Eisenhower used the parole provision to admit thirty-two thousand Hungarians. Between 1962 and 1981, more than eight hundred thousand Cubans were paroled into the United States. After the Vietnam War, Presidents Ford and Carter used their parole powers to admit hundreds of thousands of Indochinese refugees. In each of those cases, the American president acted decisively to admit refugees fleeing a regime the United States opposed.

But even as the Vietnamese and Cambodians arrived, the pressure to restrict the overall flow of immigration was building. By the 1970s, the golden years of an ever-expanding economy had been replaced by an age of limits in which Americans found themselves trying to protect their standard of living from the ravages of inflation and unemployment. Bad as it was for Americans, the bite of the global recession was even more painful for the citizens of Third World nations.

In numbers greater than at any time since the turn of the century, they sought relief in the United States. The INS apprehended an average of two hundred thousand illegal aliens annually between 1965 and 1969. In 1976, that number had quadrupled. A year later, it reached one million. In any of those years, the aliens apprehended were only a fraction of the actual number crossing the border.

The American public's frustration with this influx of foreigners was sometimes even directed at former allies. Following the fall of Saigon in 1975, polls indicated that the majority of Americans opposed resettling Vietnamese refugees in this country. Many believed they would take jobs from Americans. Still, hundreds of thousands of the Indochinese boat people came. Most were able peacefully to find a place for themselves, but a few, such as the Vietnamese fishermen who settled on Texas's Gulf Coast, found themselves facing the white robes of the Ku Klux Klan.

By 1980, the INS and the Census Bureau were speculating that between three and six million illegal aliens lived in the United States. Many came from Mexico and other Latin American nations. Scholars and government officials could not seem to decide what this meant for our society. Did the aliens, most of them young, unskilled men, take jobs that would otherwise go to U.S. citizens or did they simply accept work Americans didn't want? Were they a drain on health and educational facilities or did they pay their own way through taxes?

One thing was certain, The illegal aliens were an easily exploitable underclass that lived outside the legal protections of our system. As such, they were a threat to the system itself. "Not only do they suffer, but so too does U.S. society," the U.S. Select Commission on Immigration and Refugee Policy reported in 1981. "The presence of a substantial number of undocumented/illegal aliens in the United States has resulted not only in a disregard for immigration law but in the breaking of minimum wage and occupational safety laws, and statutes against smuggling as well. As long as undocumented migration flouts U.S. immigration, its most devastating impact may be the disregard it breeds for other U.S. laws."

The commission was an outgrowth of Jimmy Carter's attempts to overhaul the nation's immigration law. Soon after taking office in 1977, Carter proposed a plan that would have granted amnesty to millions of aliens already in the country, penalized employers for hiring illegal aliens, and replaced the Border Patrol with another agency under the control of the Treasury Department. But immigration reform was a complex and delicate issue. Organized labor might complain that the illegal aliens took jobs from American workers, but many big business interests with substantial Capitol Hill clout profited from having such a large pool of foreigners willing to work for low wages. At any rate, it was not a subject that captured the imagination of Congress, and the so-called Carter Plan was forgotten as quickly as the headlines announcing it.

Congress did, however, approve one significant piece of immigration legislation, the Refugee Act of 1980. The act increased the number of authorized admissions from 17,400 to 50,000 and required the attorney general to develop procedures for granting asylum. More important, the act brought the United States' legal definition of a refugee into line with the United Nations Protocol Relating to the Status of Refugees, which the United States had signed in 1968.

Prior to the act, U.S. law only recognized refugees fleeing Communist countries or the Middle East. The new law defined a refugee as someone fleeing a country in which he or she was persecuted or had a well-founded fear of persecution because of race, religion, nationality, political opinion, or membership in a particular social group. Under the UN protocol, a nation could not deport refugees who met this definition except for reasons of national security or public safety.

The provisions of the new law were quickly tested as immigration became a hot topic on Capitol Hill during Carter's final year in office. It was not the American president who raised the issue, but the bearded leader of a Caribbean island ninety miles off the Florida coast. In April 1980, 10,000 asylum-seeking Cubans poured into the grounds of the Peruvian embassy in Havana. Carter agreed to accept 3,500 of them in the United States. Cuban premier Fidel Castro responded by sending his disgruntled subjects off from the port of Mariel. But he did not stop with the 3,500 Cubans from the Peruvian embassy. Over the next few weeks, Castro sent 125,000 Cubans sailing off to South Florida aboard a makeshift fleet of American fishing boats and pleasure craft.

Although Carter initially threatened to fine boat captains who brought the refugees to Florida, he later announced that the United States would welcome the Cubans. But Carter did not admit them under the provisions of the new refugee act. Instead, he used his discretionary powers to parole them into the country.

It quickly became apparent that the parolees were not all here because of their opposition to Castro. INS and FBI personnel interviewing the incoming refugees found that in addition to ridding himself of thousands of political opponents, Castro had also saddled the Carter administration with up to forty thousand criminals, homosexuals, and mental patients.

In Miami, where many of them settled, the rate of burglary and violent crime soared. Cubans detained at Fort Chaffe,

Arkansas, rioted and burned four of the barracks used to house them. The majority of the Cubans were law-abiding people, but they found their future stained by the crime and unrest. The warm welcome with which the Marielitos had been greeted quickly turned to hostility.

Even as the Carter administration was struggling to cope with the Marielitos from Cuba, thousands of Haitians were wading ashore on the beaches of South Florida. In their rickety sailboats, they had been fleeing the poverty and violence of Jean-Claude Duvalier's Haiti since the early seventies. Many found refuge and work in the Bahamas, but in 1978 the government there, in hopes of easing unemployment among its own people, began expelling the Haitians. Nearly twenty-five thousand of them sought asylum in South Florida.

The treatment received by the Haitians foreshadowed what would later happen to the refugees from El Salvador and Guatemala. For a time, the Haitians were paroled into the United States with the Cubans, but that status was quickly lifted. Haitians caught by the INS soon found themselves imprisoned in squalid, makeshift detention centers. Many were sent back to Haiti, where President-for-Life Duvalier had a special police force, the Tontons Macoutes, to deal with people who were dissatisfied with his brutal rule. But the United States was hesitant to criticize Duvalier's well-documented human rights abuses. The plump dictator was a friend of the United States. Being so close to Cuba, his island-nation was also of particular strategic importance.

After he took office in 1981, Ronald Reagan directed the Coast Guard to stop the Haitian's boats on the open seas and turn them back. The interdiction order was part of the overall immigration program the Reagan administration unveiled in July 1981.

"We have lost control of our borders," Attorney General William French Smith said in announcing it. Taking a cue from the Carter Plan, Reagan proposed that employers be prohibited from hiring illegal aliens and suggested fines for those who did. The president also asked Congress to appropriate $40 million to hire additional Border Patrol agents and construct detention facilities. Noting that asylum applications had jumped from 3,800 in 1978 to 19,500 in 1980, Smith announced that the administration hoped to come up with a streamlined procedure for deciding asylum cases.

"Our nation is a nation of immigrants," the president said. "More than any other country, our strength comes from our own immigrant heritage and our capacity to welcome those from other lands." But following his glowing invocation of history, the president added a sentence indicating the new limits he envisioned for that capacity. "No free and prosperous nation can by itself accommodate all those who seek a better life or face persecution," he said.

With the Haitians, the Salvadorans were among the first groups of refugees to find out just how unaccommodating the new administration planned to be.

By the time Ronald Reagan took office, the war in El Salvador was snuffing out the lives of more than 500 civilians each month. Salvadorans were entering the United States in unprecedented numbers. During the fiscal year ending in September 1980, the INS apprehended 11,792 Salvadorans. Four years earlier, the number had been below 8,000. Border Patrol officials estimated that for every illegal alien they caught, between two and five got past them.

The Central Americans presented the INS with special problems. Before they were deported and flown home, they had to be housed. In Port Isabel, Texas, and El Centro, California, they were crowded into detention camps. The size of the Salvadoran influx taxed these facilities far beyond their limits. "It's getting to the point where it's hard to handle them all," McAllen Border Patrol chief Larry Richardson told David McLemore of the *Dallas Morning News*. "Every jail in the Rio Grande Valley is filled, and we've had to send them up to jails in Corpus Christi, San Antonio and Galveston."

Because of the violence in El Salvador, during the closing months of the Carter administration, the State Department's Human Rights Office had endorsed a plan to allow the Salvadorans to remain in this country temporarily. Carter never adopted the proposal, but just before leaving office, he did place a ninety-day freeze on processing Salvadoran asylum requests. In effect, the moratorium granted temporary refuge to about one thousand Salvadorans who had applied for asylum.

Ronald Reagan chose not to renew the freeze. Salvadorans who applied for asylum under his administration were routinely denied it. During fiscal year 1983 the United States granted political asylum to 163 Salvadorans. The status was denied to 6,576. Many were never told that under U.S. law, they had a right to apply for asylum. In Brownsville, Texas, a federal judge had to order local INS officials to do so. Meanwhile, Salvadorans were being deported at the rate of about 1,000 per month.

In late 1982, the *Brownsville* (Texas) *Herald* sent a reporter to the INS detention center in nearby Port Isabel, to interview Salvadorans being held there. Among those he met was nineteen-year-old José Hernández, a former Salvadoran soldier. After being wounded in battle, Hernández had returned to his home in San Miguel to recuperate. When guerrillas in the area threatened his family, he fled to the United States.

Hernández and twenty-five other Salvadorans paid a group of smugglers to get them into the United States. On October 4, 1982, INS investigators found most of them locked inside the airtight compartment of a refrigerator truck parked near Edinburg, Texas. Four had suffocated in the heat. José Hernández, like the other survivors, was arrested and held for deportation.

"I'm scared," Hernández told the *Herald* reporter. "I know the guerrillas are looking for me. But I guess this is God's will. He knows what He is doing and why He does it."

After Hernández was deported, his attorney, Linda Yáñez of Brownsville, went to Washington to meet with Elliot Abrams and other federal officials. Yáñez, who had represented many Salvadorans in the Rio Grande Valley, tried unsuccessfully to convince them that the Salvadorans such as Hernández should not be deported.

While she was in Washington, a letter arrived at her Brownsville office from José Hernández's brother, who was living in Houston. The letter said that two weeks after his return to El Salvador, José Hernández had been shot and decapitated outside his home. Attached to the letter was a photo of Hernández inside his open coffin. A strip of white cloth held his head to his body.

The administration's response to such stories was that it could find no evidence that Salvadorans returned to their country faced any greater risk there than anyone else. At one point, the U.S. Embassy in San Salvador tried to track down five hundred refugees who had been deported to El Salvador. Administration officials took great pride in the fact that they had been able to find roughly 50 percent of them. "Some groups argue that illegal aliens who are sent back to El Salvador meet persecution and often death," Abrams told a congressional subcommittee. "Obviously we do not believe these claims or we would not deport these people."

In a 1984 report, the Amercian Civil Liberties Union documented the cases of five refugees who had been murdered on their return to El Salvador. Despite the frantic claims of some refugee advocates in the United States and rumors among the refugees themselves, those murders did not occur on the refugees' arrival at the San Salvador International Airport. Instead, the refugees disappeared after they had returned to their home villages. To the military commanders, a person who fled the country either had something to hide or did not support the government. Some guerrilla leaders felt the same way. In revolutionary El Salvador, neither side put much stock in stern warnings or probated sentences.

Back in the United States, Reagan administration officials promised that those Salvadorans who could prove they faced such persecution back home could apply for political asylum in the United States. Of course, their chances of getting it were not good. During fiscal year 1983, the INS granted political asylum in about 30 percent of the cases it decided. Iranian applicants fleeing the Ayatollah Khomeini got favorable decisions 71 percent of the time. Sixty-two percent of those running from the Soviet-puppet regime in Afghanistan were successful. Polish and Ethiopian applicants, also fleeing Communist governments, were successful a little over 25 percent of the time. In contrast, fewer than 3 percent of the Salvadoran applicants were granted asylum.

One problem was that, other than their own affidavits, the

Central American asylum applicants seldom had documents to prove their cases. The death squads sometimes published the names of future victims in the San Salvador papers, but it was more common for them to leave their calling card after a murder. Some unions and political groups were so persecuted that mere membership in one helped an asylum plea, but having a few friends or neighbors done in was not enough.

If there was a bright spot in this for the Salvadoran asylum applicant it was that, by the end of fiscal year 1983, the INS had a backlog of 170,000 asylum cases. That meant that, with appeals, an asylum case might float in limbo for two years or more. Eventually, however, the system would catch up and for most applicants, that meant an order of deportation.

The office of the United Nations High Commissioner for Refugees (UNHCR) tried to persuade the Reagan administration to change its policy. UNHCR representatives monitoring U.S. treatment of Salvadoran refugees recommended that the agency "continue to express its concern to the U.S. government that its apparent failure to grant asylum to any significant number of Salvadorans, coupled with continuing large-scale forcible and voluntary return to El Salvador, would appear to represent a negation of its responsiblities assumed upon its adherence to the Protocol."

Some administration critics argued that, at the very least, the Salvadorans deserved Extended Voluntary Departure (EVD) status. EVD allows citizens of a country experiencing war or social upheaval to remain in the United States until hostilities are over. The attorney general has the authority to grant the status upon the recommendation of the State Department. Since 1960, the United States had given EVD to refugees from over a dozen countries. Cubans got it after Castro's victory. Czechoslovakians were given temporary refuge after Russian troops marched into their country in 1968. EVD had also been granted to refugees from Cambodia (1975), Vietnam (1975), Laos (1975), Lebanon (1976), Uganda (1978), Iran (1979), Nicaragua (1979), Afghanistan (1980), and Poland (1980).

In April 1981, Sen. Edward Kennedy asked the State Department to recommend EVD to Salvadorans. A few months later, the United States Catholic Conference became the first of many church groups to join the call. In 1983, Congress passed a non-binding resolution that the deportation of Salvadorans be halted until conditions improved in their country.

Elliot Abrams responded to the requests in an August 5, 1983, opinion piece written for the *New York Times*. Although allowing that El Salvador was a "poor and violent country in which few Americans would chose to live," Abrams argued that most Salvadorans in the United States were "not refugees fleeing persecution but would-be immigrants who want to live here. There are dozens of wars, civil wars and insurgencies in the world today, and almost all are in the third world. This violence combines with poverty as an incentive for would-be migrants to head for new jobs and homes in a rich industrial country. Those who ask that all Salvadoran migrants be allowed to stay in the United States indefinitely must explain why the same treatment is not deserved by all other migrants from the poor, violent societies to our south—now and in the coming years."

During an appearance before a House subcommitee in June 1984, Abrams asserted that the Reagan administration had no specific asylum policy for Salvadorans. They were, he said, treated like everyone else. As for EVD, Abrams said such decisions require "a balancing of judgments about their foreign policy, humanitarian and immigration policy implications."

> In the case of El Salvador, the immigration policy implications of suspension of deportation are enormous. . . . Can anyone doubt that a suspension of deportation would increase the amount of illegal immigration from El Salvador to the United States? An intelligent and industrious Salvadoran weighing a decision to try illegal immigration to the United States knows that one of the risks is deportation, which might occur before he has had a chance to earn back the costs of the journey. If we remove the possibility of deportation, it is simple logic to suggest that illegal entry become a more attractive investment.

As was his style, Abrams spent very little time that day talking about human rights abuses in El Salvador. He chose, instead, to focus on economics. Even as Abrams was carrying on the debate

in banker's terms, the stage was being set for the first court confrontation between the federal government and the sanctuary
movement. The setting was not Tucson, Chicago, San Francisco,
or any of the other of the large cities where the movement was
active. Instead, the government chose to make its first stand in a
tiny Texas town a few miles from the Rio Grande.

7

Death and Refuge in Texas

Priests met the four coffins at the door of the brick church. Father Gus Kennedy, a bearded young Bostonian, sprinkled them with holy water and said, "Praise be to God, the Father of our Lord Jesus Christ, the Father of mercies and the God of all consolation." Kennedy then turned and walked toward the altar with the bodies of four teenagers he had never known.

None of the mourners crowded into the Sacred Heart Catholic Church had ever met them. Yet on a humid Friday afternoon near the Mexican border, six hundred people from tiny Edinburg, Texas, and surrounding towns had come to pay their last respects to María Luisa Merlos Gutiérrez, Mario David Pléitez, Antonio Vidal Cruz, and Noé Fernando Espinal Flores. All teenagers. All from El Salvador.

The first anyone in town knew of them was the previous Monday, October 4, 1982. Late that night, a woman was driving down U.S. Highway 281, the main road between Edinburg and the Mexican border. A few miles south of town, she passed a tractor-trailer rig parked near an overpass. The back door of the big refrigerator truck was open. There was a body on the ground nearby. The motorist called the sheriff's department. It looked like an accident.

Edinburg fire chief Johnny Economedes was one of the first to arrive at the scene. The man he found lying outside the truck was dead. Of the fifteen people inside the trailer, three were dead and twelve were suffering from severe dehydration. Some were unconscious, others were too weak to stand. "They were so hot it was like they were on fire," Economedes told a reporter. "They were pretty well cooked."

While the survivors were rushed to area hospitals, the bodies of the dead were taken to a funeral home in nearby Pharr. Father Kennedy went there the following day to bless them. The doctor who conducted the autopsies ruled that the four teenagers had died of suffocation and heat stroke. By that time, investigators had begun interviewing survivors and piecing together what had happened.

The four dead teenagers had been part of a group of fifty Salvadorans who had left their country a week earlier in a chartered bus. Each of them had paid their professional smuggler or "coyote," $1,500 to get them to Houston, New York, Washington, and other U.S. cities. In between Central America and the U.S. border lay more than a thousand miles of Mexico, but corruption there was so dependable, a coyote could plan to bribe his way through with a busload of undocumented aliens.

The Salvadorans arrived on the border at Reynosa, Mexico, on Sunday, October 3. They were divided into two groups. There were twenty-six in the one that included the four teenagers. Sometime Sunday night, a Mexican guide led them across the Rio Grande to the refrigerator truck waiting on the other side. After the Salvadorans had gone into the trailer, the doors were locked from the outside. At that point, the airtight trailer's ventilation system was still working.

On Monday, the smugglers drove the truck to the spot on U.S. Highway 281 and parked it, apparently waiting until dark to drive their human cargo through the Border Patrol roadblocks along the handful of highways leading north out of the valley. They brought the Salvadorans food and water once during the day, then locked the trailer again and left.

That afternoon, as the temperature outside inched past ninety degrees, the truck's ventilation system failed. The Salvadorans began shedding their clothes to stay cool. Heat was not their only problem. With the ventilation system down, they had no fresh air. Some of the refugees tore at the inside of the truck with their hands. They managed to rip away a few wall panels and some insulation, but not to break through to the outside. Instead, they spent the afternoon sweating and choking on the fiery hot air that remained.

When the smugglers returned that night, they opened the truck doors to find that four of their passengers had died. Most of the others could barely move. The ten still able to walk were loaded into a smaller van and dropped in an orange grove a few miles away. Many were wearing only their underwear. They were captured by the Border Patrol after going to nearby homes to beg for clothing.

Although the smugglers left the truck door unlocked the second time, the remaining Salvadorans lacked the strength to leave it. "Things must be pretty bad over there to make these people go to these lengths to try to go to America," said one state trooper.

Two of the bodies were to be shipped back to El Salvador, but Antonio Vidal Cruz and Noé Fernando Espinal Flores were to be buried in the country they had known only in death. At the Valley Memorial Cemetery, one of the North Americans held the blue and white flag of El Salvador as Father Kennedy asked God for comfort. "They were nourished with your body and blood," he prayed. "Grant them a place at the table in your heavenly kingdom."

When the graveside service had ended, the Rev. Ralph Baumgartner, a local Lutheran pastor, stepped forward. "It's the people who are victims of this horrible war," said Baumgartner, spokesman for the Border Association for Refugees from Central America. "They live without certainty of knowing whether they can go on from one day to the next. So they flee for refuge," he said. "It comes to this."

By the time of the Edinburg tragedy, churches in Tucson and San Francisco had been sanctuaries for six months. Thousands of Central American refugees were entering the Rio Grande Valley of Texas, which, by land, was closer to Guatemala and El Salvador than were Arizona, California, or any other part of the United States. Yet there had not been a single sanctuary declaration in South Texas. Nor would there be.

Unlike Tucson, home of the University of Arizona, or San

Francisco, with its longstanding liberal tradition, the Rio Grande Valley is a deeply conservative place. In some ways, its history resembles that of Central America more than other parts of the United States. Until recent times, Anglo cattle barons and ranchers had dominated its economy. They owned vast stretches of the Valley and hired Mexicans from across the river to work for them. The Mexicans worked cheap, lived miserably, and were treated with all the respect some whites in other parts of the South gave blacks. Those Mexicans who did gain U.S. citizenship often became pawns in a border version of Chicago-style machine politics.

By the 1980s, many of the descendants of those early Mexican workers had become part of the growing middle class in the Valley, but it remained an area where old traditions hung on. One reason was isolation. Even with the construction of four-lane highways, the Valley was still a five-hour drive from San Antonio, the nearest big city.

Smuggling also had a long tradition in the Valley. North Americans airlifted everything from guns to color televisions into Mexico. They, along with their counterparts across the border, smuggled Mexican marijuana and South American cocaine to an eager American public.

Smugglers specializing in human contraband were known as "coyotes." Large and often well-armed rings of them operated with virtual impunity in Mexico, using a portion of their income to salt the pockets of Mexican politicians and police. For transportation, they maintained fleets of cars and trucks, many of them stolen, on the U.S. side of the border. They also kept safe houses in border towns from El Paso to Brownsville. Aliens were sometimes hidden there temporarily until they could be transported away from the border.

Although the Border Patrol knew how the smuggling rings operated, it had never possessed the manpower to stop them. Instead, government agents and smugglers played a cat-and-mouse game along the banks of the river. Border Patrol surveillance was heaviest within a twenty-mile strip of land adjacent to the Rio Grande. Agents watched popular crossings and a system of electronic sensors monitored movement along the riverbanks. Plain-clothes officers were posted in the bus stations and airports of Brownsville, Harlingen, and McAllen. Roadblocks were maintained on U.S. Highways 77 and 281, the main routes out of the Valley. The agency's light green cruisers patroled other roads and its small planes watched for aliens trying to make their way north through the rugged brush. Getting into the United States was one thing. Getting out of the Valley was another.

Still, most coyotes managed to find a way. Aliens were strapped under cars, jammed into house trailers, or stuffed into trucks. For the smugglers, the money was too good to resist. "Smuggling is just about the best business there is," Larry Richardson, former chief of the Border Patrol's McAllen sector told David McLemore of the *Dallas Morning News*. "You got a cargo that will come to you, pay you money and lie for you if you get caught. A lot of dope smugglers are getting into the illegal alien game because it's safer and very lucrative."

The Valley was one of the most popular points of entry for Central American refugees. The Border Patrol office in McAllen caught 711 Salvadorans in 1978. By 1980, the year following the start of the Salvadoran civil war, the number of apprehensions had increased to 1,754. The Border Patrol estimated it was only catching about one quarter of them.

The slums and cheap hotels of the Mexican border towns such as Matamoros and Reynosa were filled with Central Americans waiting for their chance to cross the muddy Rio Grande. They had traveled the length of Mexico on foot and by bus, paying bribes to Mexican authorities along the way. Many were broke by the time they reach the border and had no choice but to wade or swim the Rio Grande on their own. Others sought the help of coyotes.

The Central Americans presented the smugglers with profitable new opportunities. Because they did not know the territory, they were more often at the coyote's mercy. Knowing this, the coyotes routinely doubled the rates they charge for Mexicans. The refugees paid from $300 to $2,000 to be taken across, depending on their destination and the mood of the coyote. To pay the cost of the passage, many refugees had sold their homes and possessions.

But even the high prices were no guarantee that refugees would be taken to their destination. During the 1981 Memorial Day weekend, the Border Patrol captured eight Salvadorans who had been abandoned in a cornfield west of Brownsville. They had no food, no water, and no idea of where they were. Later that week, agents found thirty-three refugees who had been locked inside an old Post Office truck. In July 1982, the bodies of four Salvadorans were found near the Brazos River in Fort Bend County, Texas. They had been murdered after their relatives were unable to pay coyotes a ransom for their release.

The Border Patrol was not prepared to deal with the growing number of Central Americans, or OTM's (Other than Mexicans), as they called them. Unlike the aliens from Mexico, the Central Americans could not simply be loaded onto a bus and dropped off on the other side of the nearest international bridge. They have to be flown home. Some fought deportation by applying for political asylum. Even those who opted for voluntary departure had to be fed and housed while their papers are processed.

That meant a stay at the INS processing center west of Port Isabel. Central Americans referred to the one hundred-acre facility as "El Corralón," the big corral. Formerly a naval air station, El Corralón was an inhospitable collection of chain link fences and low-slung dormitories. It was a few miles inland from Port Isabel, on the hot coastal plains of South Texas. During the day, detainees stayed in the dusty and shadeless "recreation yard." Although an expansion would eventually increase El Corralón's capacity to nearly seven hundred, when the first wave of Central Americans began arriving, there was room for only about one-third that many. The rest were put up in motels, churches, and county jails as far away as Galveston and San Antonio.

Aliens remained in detention until they were deported or bonded out. With the help of an immigration lawyer, an alien could get a $10,000 bond reduced to $3,000. Usually, the local bonding companies required about $750 of that amount in cash. The money often came from Valley churches.

Many of these churches had aided undocumented aliens from Mexico. By 1980, priests, pastors, and nuns who worked with

Mexican aliens began encountering more and more Central Americans during their visits to El Corralón and area jails. They also met the new arrivals at the church doors, where many of them went for help.

In August 1981, a study of Central American refugees in the Valley was written for the *Texas Observer,* a well-respected liberal journal based in Austin. The authors were Joe Feagin, a University of Texas sociology professor, and Chad Richardson, a sociology professor at Pan American University in Edinburg. The report was sympathetic toward the refugees' plight and critical of the U.S. government's refusal to grant them political asylum. Not long after the article was published, Richardson gathered a small group of clergymen, nuns, lay people, and college professors together at Pan American University and formed the Border Association for Refugees from Central America (BARCA).

In the months that followed, BARCA became the refugees' main advocate in the Valley. In addition to raising bond money and finding attorneys, BARCA provided the refugees with food, shelter, and housing. Although BARCA leaders tried to spread the word about the plight of the refugees, their tactics were usually less confrontational than those of their counterparts in Tucson. "The area is very conservative, so we didn't want to do anything that would close the people to their [the refugees'] witness," explained BARCA director Ninfa Krueger.

Twenty miles to the east, in Harlingen, attorney Lisa Brodyaga founded Proyecto Libertad (Project Liberty). The Catholic University graduate had moved to the Valley in 1977 to provide legal services to farm workers. In her work, she too began meeting the Salvadorans and Guatemalans.

In a battered old house in downtown Harlingen, Brodyaga assembled a small staff of attorneys, volunteers, and Salvadoran paralegals. Money was so scarce that some of the staff lived at the office. Most of the funds that were available from churches, foundations, and private donations went into a long series of legal battles with the INS. Sometimes the work was as simple as getting a bond reduced. In other instances, Brodyaga and the others argued the merits of political asylum cases, all the while knowing that the application would probably be denied. Most of the time, it was just a matter of buying time. "We try to keep them here as long as possible and hope that the situation improves," said paralegal Norman Plotkin. "It's a game of delay."

BARCA and Proyecto Libertad were the exceptions. Despite articles in the local papers, most Valley residents paid little attention to the Central Americans. Not even the Edinburg tragedy changed that. But the deaths of the four teenagers did strengthen the commitment of those who were already working with the refugees. It also persuaded Bishop John Fitzpatrick of Brownsville to take up their cause.

Before coming to Texas in 1971, the Buffalo native had spent twenty-three years in South Florida. When Cuban refugees began arriving in Miami following Fidel Castro's 1959 takeover, the archbishop of Miami put Fitzpatrick in charge of the church's refugee program. There was, however, a major difference between Miami in 1961 and Brownsville twenty years later. The United States had welcomed the Cubans as political refugees fleeing a communist regime. The Central Americans were turned back.

Soon after the deaths of the four teenagers, Fitzpatrick got a visit from Rosemary Smith, a church social worker from Cleveland, Ohio. Smith had worked with the poor in El Salvador for sixteen years before the National Guard there killed four of her coworkers in December 1980. The four American churchwomen were raped and murdered after their van was stopped by a group of National Guardsmen outside San Salvador's international airport on the night on December 2, 1980. Their bodies were discovered in a roadside grave two days later.

Rosemary Smith was visiting the United States when the murders occurred. On the advice of friends, she did not return to El Salvador. But neither did she forget it. Instead, Smith went to the Rio Grande Valley to work with Salvadoran refugees. She told Bishop Fitzpatrick that people as desperate as those in the refrigerator truck needed a safe haven. Smith did not propose a permanent sanctuary like the Presbyterians had opened in Tucson, but a way station where refugees could rest from their journeys and prepare for whatever lay ahead. With the funerals of the four teenagers still fresh in his mind, the bishop agreed.

As the site, they chose a four-room house in San Benito, a town of eighteen thousand about twenty miles north of Brownsville. St. Benedict's Catholic Church there had used the little white stucco building as a classroom. It was in the midst of a Mexican-American neighborhood just off U.S. Highway 77, a route many refugees followed to get out of the Valley.

Smith became the shelter's first director. The church named it for the Salvadoran archbishop who had been assassinated two years earlier. Casa Oscar Romero opened on December 2, 1982, the second anniversary of the murders of Rosemary Smith's friends in El Salvador. At the dedication ceremony, Bishop Fitzpatrick said that, although the United States government did not welcome the Central Americans as refugees, the church had a Christian duty to care for people who were without food, clothing, or shelter.

The local INS director was notified of the new facility. If he saw it as a threat to federal law enforcement, he gave no sign. In fact, many of the Casa's first lodgers were refugees the INS had apprehended but could not house at the Port Isabel detention center. Border Patrol agents began dropping them off for safekeeping at the Casa while their cases were processed. The agents told Smith that refugees who had come to the shelter on their own had to turn themselves in to the INS, but they never made any effort to question new arrivals.

"That was a woman from Pharr," Rosemary Smith said after hanging up the phone. "She had three Salvadorans come to her house looking for help. Usually when they come, they look for a church," the gray-haired woman added as she eased herself into an old chair near the picture window of her paneled living room. The trailer window looked out onto a small covered porch and a broad field of parched grass. Just to the left of the dusty drive that led to the trailer, a half-dozen young men were playing volleyball in the yard.

By June 1983, Smith had been living in the trailer behind Casa Oscar Romero for a little more than six months. With a few volunteers, she tended to the Central Americans who came to

Casa Oscar Romero, which was just across the field. Within three years, one hundred to two hundred refugees a night would crowd into the little shelter, but in the summer of 1983, there were usually no more than a dozen or so. They came to the Casa from Guatemala, Honduras, and Nicaragua, but the largest percentage were Salvadorans. Most were young men — army deserters, ex-guerrillas, farmers fleeing the fight. Although some remained suspicious of each other, they seldom renewed their hostilities at the Casa. For Smith, the bigger problem was ejecting those who occasionally sneaked away to get drunk.

In 1983, women were still a rarity at the Casa, although they arrived from time to time. For them, the journey was often more dangerous. "I had one fourteen-year-old girl here who was raped by two of the immigration people in Mexico," Smith said, without a hint of surprise in her voice.

Few of the refugees stayed at the Casa for more than two weeks. Some drifted off on their own. Many filed for asylum with the INS in the Valley and then had their cases transferred to cities where relatives lived. Although the chances of getting asylum were slim, the slow appeals process might permit them to stay in the United States for two years or more. Some Salvadorans applied for asylum in Canada, which was more willing to recognize them as political refugees. The Canadian consul from Dallas frequently visited the Valley to interview Salvadorans for possible relocation in Canada. Although the asylum candidates were given resettlement money, the Canadian government was selective about whom it accepted.

Still, Smith explained, most of the refugees arrived at Casa Romero thinking they had reached the promised land. "They all seem to think that once they are here, they can get permission to stay," she said. "The minute they come, they ask us to get them permission."

The volleyball players were gone by the time Smith led the way to the Casa a few minutes later. Between her trailer and the house was a small garden where the refugees had planted corn and tomatoes. A thick wooden table sat in the backyard. T-shirts and socks hung from a clothesline attached to the house.

Inside the Casa, a cauldron of pinto beans simmered on the

stovetop. A few bags of corn sat on the counter waiting to be husked. A chart on the kitchen wall listed the chores for those staying at the Casa.

The two bedrooms were lit by bare overhead bulbs. Second-hand beds and bunks built of plywood and two-by-fours lined the walls of the two bedrooms. A black-and-white TV flickered at one end of the larger room. Beside it was the pay phone refugees used to call home. At the other side of the room, a blackboard was set up beside a table. Those men who had not found jobs on one of the nearby farms were getting an English lesson from a Casa volunteer.

Eduardo and his nephew Raúl were among the men staying at the Casa. Eduardo was a small man. His graying hair and double chin made him appear older than twenty-four. Like his father, he had worked in the cornfields near Nueva Esparta, a small village near the Honduran border. He had hopes of a better life, though, and so, when he became a bit older, Eduardo moved to San Salvador and got a job at the airport.

After the war broke out, the army began sending him draft notices. Four times, Eduardo paid the local commander a $20 bribe to avoid service. Finally, after receiving a letter saying that young men such as him were traitors, Eduardo decided it was time to join the army.

For thirteen months, he and his unit guarded a government radio tower outside San Miguel, a city in the embattled eastern region of El Salvador. When some weapons disappeared from the local armory, Eduardo and five fellow soldiers were accused of giving them to the guerillas. They were arrested and told they would be executed by a firing squad.

In the military prison, Eduardo learned that two of his fellow soldiers were in fact guerillas who had infiltrated the army, but the information did not help him prove his own innocence. Instead, he was interrogated for forty-five days. The sessions included electric shocks and the *capuche,* an airtight hood dusted with lime and then slipped over the victim's head.

Eduardo and the others decided to escape. One rainy night as their guard slept, they dug through the soft prison walls. Eduardo was the last to go. By the time he dropped to the ground, he could hear guards chasing the others. Hunched there beside the prison wall, he looked up to see a soldier pointing a machine gun at him. It was an old friend from Nueva Esparta. He looked around quickly, then motioned for Eduardo to run.

The escaped prisoner took a bus to the Honduran border, slipped across, and applied for political asylum. The government ordered him out of the country, warning that, if he returned, they would turn him over to Salvadoran authorities.

Eduardo went to Panama and Costa Rica looking for work but found none. After two years living as a beggar, he decided to risk going home. In Nueva Esparta, his father was shocked to see him. The family had assumed he was dead. But the reunion did not last long. A few days after Eduardo arrived, the army came looking for him. He escaped through the back door as the soldiers were coming down the street.

He hitchhiked to a relative's home in San Salvador. His nephew, just two years younger, was already there. Raúl was on the run, too, but for different reasons.

The younger man was also from Nuevo Esparta, where he had worked at a plant that made cement mixers. Unlike his uncle, Raúl was very involved with politics. He regularly made trips to San Salvador to take part in demonstrations against the government. During one demonstration, he was wounded in the back by a police bullet.

Raúl was also part of a group of workers trying to start a labor union at their factory in Nueva Esparta. They continued their organizing, despite frequent threats from right-wing death squads. One day, while Raúl was working beside a man doing some soldering, a group of thugs entered the plant. They grabbed Raúl's coworker, ripped off his goggles, and thrust the hot soldering iron into his eye. This was meant as a warning to the other workers.

Instead of being intimidated into silence, Raúl left his job and joined the guerrillas. He spent a year living in the hills and fighting skirmishes with the Salvadoran Army. Then he heard that, because of his activity, the security forces had threatened his mother back in Nueva Esparta. Hoping to ease the pressure on her, he laid down his weapon one night and slipped out of the guerrilla camp.

He was hiding at a relative's home in San Salvador when his uncle Eduardo arrived. They went to Mexico City, where they worked for a few months to earn enough money to pay a coyote to smuggle them into Texas. At Casa Oscar Romero, both men applied for political asylum in Canada. Eduardo was accepted. Because he had fought for the guerrillas, Raúl was not. In June 1983, while Eduardo made plans to settle in Edmonton, Alberta, Raúl spent his days at Casa Oscar Romero, pondering his options.

He doubted the United States would give asylum to a former guerrilla or that his government would welcome him back. He might try to slip out of the Valley on his own, but there was a good chance the Border Patrol would catch him. By that time, though, there was another possibility for Raúl and other Salvadorans to consider.

8

A Ride Into the Promised Land

The sun had only been in the pale blue Valley sky for an hour, but already the tiny Texas border town was blanketed with a heavy, dead heat. On such a day just walking out to get the morning paper was enough to work up a sweat. And it was only June.

In the rectory of a little church not far from the square, I watched as a sixteen-year-old named Miguel sat poking at a breakfast of fruit rolls and coffee laced with milk. He was a small boy with smooth olive skin and a thick mop of black hair. Dressed in a yellow baseball cap, t-shirt, and faded jeans, Miguel could have been a young outfielder ready for a day on some dusty sandlot diamond. Surely on such a summer day there were South Texas boys waking up thinking of baseball. And of afternoons on the beaches of nearby Padre Island. And of cruising the shopping malls of Brownsville and Harlingen. And of girls. But none of this was on Miguel's mind. He had no idea of where the ballfields, malls, or girls were.

Miguel was a stranger in town and something of a fugitive as well. Even as he munched his sweet roll, the light green Border Patrol cruisers were patrolling the highways of the Valley looking for young men like him. Most of the ones they would catch in the freight yards and brushlands would be Mexicans just a few miles from their own border. They would be put aboard a Border Patrol bus and dropped off across the river.

It would be different for Miguel, who was Salvadoran. If he were caught, chances were he would end up on a plane bound for San Salvador. As an Army deserter, that was not a trip the boy wanted to make. He thought it might mean his death. Miguel had no proof, really, just a feeling based on his experiences with the war that had been occupying the days of sixteen-year-olds of his country.

He had come from a village near San Miguel, a city in the eastern part of El Salvador, and lately the scene of some of the heaviest fighting between the army and the guerrillas. There, Miguel knew boys who had gone off to fight for both sides. He had no desire to take up arms, but when he was fifteen, an army patrol had come through his neighborhood and rounded up all the young men. Miguel and his two brothers, ages fourteen and twenty, suddenly found themselves in uniform. Miguel had known enough not to resist. To do so was to be branded a subversive, and Miguel had seen the hacked-up corpses of many subversives being dragged from the ditches around his home.

Soon after Miguel finished his training, the rebels launched an offensive. Miguel's unit suffered heavy casualties. Although he was afraid every minute, he fought well. After one skirmish, Miguel's commander rewarded him with a pass to go home and visit his family.

He returned to his village to find the war waiting. One day the guerrillas would sweep through and push out the army. When the rebels were in control, it could be dangerous or fatal to be caught with army credentials. Then the government planes would fly over and bomb the village. Sometimes the army would regain control. During those times, young men caught without army papers were suspected of being guerrillas.

Day after day, the bombing, shooting, and killing continued. Even a veteran of battle found it hard to endure the terror and uncertainty. Having never felt that it was his war to begin with, Miguel decided to leave. He and a few friends set out on foot for the Guatemalan border, more than one hundred miles to the west. Miguel was not certain how he would make it across that mountainous country or the long stretch of Mexican highway that rolled out beyond it. But he knew of a place called Houston. He had two cousins there. They painted houses.

Miguel and his friends reached Matamoros, Mexico, a few months later. By that time, he had only $18 in his pocket. The rest had been spent on food, bus tickets, and bribes to the Mexican police. Matamoros was dirty and hot. There seemed to be Mexicans and Salvadorans everywhere who were waiting to ford the Rio Grande. The coyotes prowled the streets boasting of their skill at getting people across the river and past the Border Patrol.

With no way to raise the money for a coyote, Miguel and his friends decided to cross on their own. Although he was still uncertain of how to get to Houston, someone in Mexico had told him to go to Casa Oscar Romero in San Benito. The Casa was run by the Catholic church. He was told the people there would give him food and shelter. Perhaps they would even help him get to Houston.

Luck was with the young soldier. Late one night he was able to find a place in the brown river where the current was slow. There had not been any Border Patrol agents waiting on the other side. By staying close to the highway, he was able to find the shelter, which was in a neighborhood right beside the highway to San Antonio.

Jorge was among the Salvadorans already staying at the shelter. The thirty-three-year-old truck driver had come to Texas from San Francisco Gotera, another hard-hit Salvadoran city. Unlike his young friend, Jorge had no troubles with the draft. He had served in the Salvadoran army long before the civil war began. His problems were caused by generosity. He had given food to the government soldiers when they asked for it and he had also supplied the guerrillas when they passed through his neighborhood. Eventually, both sides became suspicious of him. Like Miguel, he had seen bodies in the streets and ditches. He too wanted to get to Houston. From there, he would catch a plane to Los Angeles, where his brother cleaned offices.

After several days at Casa Oscar Romero, the army deserter and the truck driver were having breakfast at a church and waiting for the sanctuary movement's underground railroad to take them to Houston.

In just one year, the railroad reached from Guatemala all the way to Seattle, Detroit, and Boston. The most dangerous part of the line was south of the U.S. border, where church workers accompanied the Central Americans on trains and planes through

Mexico and at times drove them past Mexican immigration checkpoints in cars.

The first spur of the railroad in the United States had been the Nogales-Tucson route in Arizona. Originally, Jim Corbett, the Rev. John Fife, and a few others had relied on luck in getting refugees up from Nogales. But over time, they learned when the Border Patrol shifts changed and what sort of profile they were looking for on the highways. By sandwiching a refugee or two between several Anglos, the cars were less likely to be stopped. The INS also seemed less suspicious of women drivers and so housewives, including some with children, became runners for the railroad. Corbett or one of the other border breakers would lead the refugees across the border, through the brush, and into what, to a casual observer, might look like a roadside picnic. Instead it would be sanctuary sympathizers waiting for their next load.

Although the Texas border was more populated, many of the same tactics worked well and by June 1983 the underground railroad was well established between the Rio Grande Valley and large Texas cities such as Austin, San Antonio, and Houston. From there, refugees might catch planes to northern cities or find other drivers willing to shuttle them to church sanctuaries deeper in the North American heartland.

Max, the clergyman, was singing when he came down the stairs. He was a muscular, energetic man in his thirties. If he was worried about his plans to break federal immigration laws that morning, he showed no sign of it.

"Are you an American citizen?" Max barked at Miguel as he poured himself coffee.

"Yup," the Salvadoran answered in his best English.

"Where are you from?"

"San Benito."

Max mussed Miguel's hair and told him he looked too much like a North American for them to be stopped. Looking up from his coffee, Jorge the truck driver smiled and said he was not so confident: Max looked too much like a Cuban.

The clergyman was taking a substantial risk by driving the two

Salvadorans out of the Valley. The penalty for transporting an illegal alien was up to five years in prison and a $2,000 fine. Max might face other charges for harboring aliens or conspiring to commit such a crime. More than that, he was not certain what his congregation would say if he were caught. In other parts of the country, churches had made decisions to become sanctuaries for Central Americans. None had in the Rio Grande Valley. In fact, Max's congregation, which included several people who worked for the Immigration and Naturalization Service, had never even discussed it. They had no idea that their pastor hid refugees in the rectory at night or that he smuggled them out of the Valley during the day.

Max explained that the deaths of the four Salvadoran youths near Edinburg the previous fall had moved him to look into the problems of Salvadoran refugees in the Rio Grande Valley. That quickly led to his involvement with the sanctuary movement and the underground railroad. "This is about as honest as you can get as far as I'm concerned," Max said, sipping coffee. "This is what the church is all about. I can't see myself sitting in the office answering phone calls all day. If that's what the gospel means to some people, it just doesn't make sense."

After a quick trip to the service station to have his battered sedan checked by a mechanic, Max returned and loaded the Salvadorans' bags into the trunk. As the clergyman and his passengers pulled into the town's main street, a few early-rising businessmen were unlocking their offices. A row of big American pickup trucks were parked outside the diner. Miguel and Jorge sat in the back seat watching the tranquil scene pass. Max pushed a cassette into his player. John Lennon sang "Imagine." Then came Elvis Presley with "How Great Thou Art," and finally Jimmy Buffett with "Changes in Latitudes, Changes in Attitudes." Max sang along, well off key.

"I'll sing louder once we make it," he promised.

The Salvadorans were to spend the night in San Antonio. Max's mission was to rendezvous with another driver at a small city midway there. Max said he did not know who the other driver would be. If stopped, he added, the less known the better.

Normally, it would take about three hours to drive to the exchange point, but Max was not taking the most direct route. Only a handful of highways lead directly north from the Valley. The Border Patrol has permanent checkpoints on some, and occasional roadblocks on others. Its cruisers are always on patrol. By zigzagging his way north on old farm roads and small-town streets, Max hoped to avoid all of them.

Miguel looked out of the window as the old sedan drove past cornfields and grazing cattle. "It looks a little like El Salvador," he said.

Jorge leaned forward to talk about the bombs he had seen fall on his town. "They don't miss because they are from the United States," he said in Spanish. He smiled, seeming to mean this as a compliment.

The car approached a Texas Department of Agriculture checkpoint where trucks leaving the Valley were checked for produce from Mexico. It was not manned, but Max hunched over the wheel and watched for Border Patrol trucks. "They could have been there," he said, looking into his rearview mirror. "By this time, we should have passed at least one. It's sort of strange."

Without turning his head, Max again demanded to know whether Miguel was an American citizen.

"Yup," the boy said, grinning. He put his head against the window and was asleep when a Border Patrol truck passed going in the opposite direction on an otherwise empty rural road. Max's hands tightened on the steering wheel again. The car was approaching a town that underground railroad drivers believed marked the end of the Border Patrol's most intense surveillance.

Max looked toward the ceiling of the car. "We're not going to get a flat, right Lord?" he said. "My car's not going to overheat? We're not going to get a flat?"

He stopped for a light in the center of town, made a right turn, and found himself behind another Border Patrol truck. Jorge nudged Miguel and pointed ahead. Max and his passengers were silent as the two vehicles went through several intersections together. The Border Patrol truck was empty except for the two agents. There was nothing to stop them from pulling Max over and taking his passengers on to El Corralón. But at one intersection, Max made a left and the Border Patrol truck continued going straight.

"Freedom!" the clergyman screamed in Spanish as the car rolled out of town. "No more. No more bombs." Still driving, he reached back to shake hands with Miguel and Jorge. "In the back of their minds," Max said to me "they must believe they're in the promised land and nothing can happen to them."

Jorge leaned forward again. That is true, he said, but both he and Miguel hope to return to El Salvador when the war is over.

"It's not going to end," Miguel said looking out the window.

Jorge was in a good mood. "In twenty years," he laughed, "they will have killed all the people and the war will end."

An hour later, Max stopped to buy hamburgers. While waiting for them, the clergyman went into a phone booth to call a coordinator in the Valley to make certain the second driver was headed south from San Antonio. In the next small town, Max pulled off the highway and into the parking lot of a church. Within five minutes, another car stopped a few feet away. Max waved to the other driver, but said nothing. The two Salvadorans retrieved their bags from his trunk and got into the second car.

The new driver said hello to her passengers, but little more. "I don't even know who they are and I don't need to know," she explained, pulling back onto the highway.

In her mid-thirties, Anna was a teacher from San Antonio, a single mother with a teenaged son. A strong-willed woman, she talked of politics when I asked why she was a driver for the railroad. After living with a family in revolutionary Nicaragua for several weeks, she came away convinced that the United States was to blame for Central America's problems.

"It's real simple for me," she explained, as Miguel and Jorge sat quietly in the back seat. "As I see it, our country is the main cause for the violence and oppression in the Central American countries. I feel like if we were not intervening in those countries' politics, the people themselves could have solved their problems.

"That makes me, as a citizen of our country, responsible," she added. "The only thing I can do to live with that is do everything against it." To do less, she said, would be akin to what the Germans did while the Jews were murdered in Nazi death camps.

Both Miguel and Jorge had fallen asleep in the sunlit back seat.

It was mid-afternoon and very hot. Cars raced by on the interstate. Anna hugged the speed limit. No need to take chances,
even though it was unlikely a car driven by an Anglo woman
would be stopped by the Border Patrol this far from the border.
Anna had been stopped a few weeks earlier on a run nearer the
Valley, but the Border Patrol agents let her go. They did, however, take her Salvadoran passengers into custody, for which she
was sorry. But as far as going to jail herself, Anna said she never
worried about it. "If you make a decision to do something, you
just have to be willing to take the consequences."

"We've had nothing to do," Miguel said the next morning as he
came from the rectory of a church in downtown San Antonio. He
was still wearing the same baseball cap, t-shirt, and jeans.

As he shut the car doors, the third and final driver explained
that it would be dangerous for them even to take a walk around
the neighborhood. They might get lost, they might get stopped by
the local police, anything could happen. "It's not worth the risk,
considering the long distance they have come," he said.

Like Anna, the driver before him, Rick asked no questions of
his passengers and made no small talk. Mostly it was out of
respect for them, he said. They had come from a country where
interrogation was often a prelude to torture. And, he added, if he
were ever stopped he could truly say that he knew nothing about
his passengers.

"You see the INS cars go by, but I've never felt a real threat,"
he added as the car rolled over a long stretch of flatland that leads
to Houston. "I think they realize we are not in it for the money,
that we don't deal with coyotes."

Although he had been interested in Central America since
college, Rick began driving for the underground railroad a few
months after hearing Jim Corbett speak in Austin in late 1982.
Like Corbett, Rick had worked bonding refugees out of detention
centers and helping them fight deportation in the courts, but that
route was expensive and time-consuming. Meanwhile, refugees

were being put on planes for El Salvador.

"You resort to civil disobedience because otherwise, you're ineffective," he said. "I would rather spend twenty bucks in gas getting these guys to Houston than put it toward a $1,000 bond."

Three hours later, the glimmering Houston skyline came into view. Jorge handed Rick a crumpled piece of paper with an address and phone number on it. Rick found the address on his street map. It turned out to be a large but shabby hotel in the center of town. No one there knew any Salvadoran truck driver named Jorge.

After a few phone calls, Rick drove to an apartment complex across town. The first door he knocked on was opened by a black woman. She was not waiting for any Jorge, but the Salvadoran in the apartment above her was.

"Delivered," said Rick, smiling for the first time. Miguel's cousin lived a few blocks away. The address he had written down was correct and after a brief farewell, the boy soldier disappeared into a small apartment building.

"It's like saying the people who cooperated with the resistance in France were irresponsible," Rick said, heading back to San Antonio. "I think we're being responsible citizens and good Christians, too."

Rick seemed satisfied with his answer, but he doubted the Border Patrol would if they ever caught him. "I still wonder what I'd say if I got stopped."

9

The Crackdown Begins

The dark sedan rolled off the exit ramp early that April afternoon in 1984. The federal marshals had no problem finding their way. The man they had come for lived in a little San Benito neighborhood beside U.S. Highway 77, one of the main north-south routes in the Rio Grande Valley of Texas. They drove west for a few blocks and then turned north onto Wentz Street. The Mexican-American neighborhood was filled with small frame houses, the sort contractors threw up by the hundreds after World War II. Just past the intersection of Wentz and Bowie streets, there was a gap in the row of homes. As the lawmen looked out across the little field there, they could see a small white stucco building called Casa Oscar Romero and behind it the trailer where first Rosemary Smith and now Jack Elder and his family lived. It was off by itself, with not so much as a tree overhead to fend off the smothering Valley heat.

The marshals looked uneasy as they walked toward the trailer. They had made arrests before, served papers, and taken men and women off to jail. Trouble was always a possibility, but no one expected Elder to throw a punch or pull a gun. That, however, did not mean there might not be a commotion. Elder and his colleagues in the sanctuary movement had been causing plenty of that for months.

That day would be no exception. When the sedan pulled up, the television crews waiting in the yard hauled out their cameras and microphones. The reporters who had been drinking under a tree across the street quickly put down their beer cans and pulled out their notebooks.

The authorities had hoped to avoid just such a spectacle. Three days earlier, on April 10, 1984, a federal grand jury in Brownsville had indicted Elder, forty, on charges of transporting illegal aliens. He was accused of taking three Salvadorans from Casa Oscar Romero — the San Benito refugee shelter he and his wife managed — to the bus station in Harlingen, about five miles to the north. After the indictment was announced, federal officials called Elder and tried to talk him into driving down to Brownsville and giving himself up.

The former San Antonio math teacher refused. In his eyes, the immigration laws were being broken by the U.S. government, not by Jack Elder. If they wanted to arrest him, they would have to come to San Benito to do so. When they did, he would see to it that the reporters were waiting.

Elder took little pleasure in publicity. By nature, the tall, bone-skinny man was a shy sort who preferred keeping to himself and to his family. But a few years earlier, he had taken on the cause of refugees from El Salvador and Guatemala. Elder had learned quickly that the news media was a tool to be employed in their behalf. He didn't mind using it, even if that meant sacrificing some privacy. It was nothing compared to what the Central Americans had lost.

Diane Elder was taking a nap when the marshals arrived. She woke up when they brought Jack back to the trailer to say good-bye to his family. The reporters tried to follow, but one of the marshals blocked the door. In the back bedroom where the whole family slept, Elder put on a shirt and kissed his wife and sons. Ten-year-old Jesse watched as an officer frisked his father and then clamped a pair of handcuffs onto his wrists.

As he was led to the car, Elder held them up for the cameras.

Jack Elder, the son of a tool-and-die maker, was born in Detroit and raised in New Haven, Connecticut. He came from a conservative Catholic family and considered himself to be the same. Elder graduated from Catholic University in 1966 with a degree in biology and with the belief that Barry Goldwater and

Richard Nixon had the true vision of America. But Elder was also something of an idealist, a man who had been moved by John Kennedy's calls for young Americans to sacrifice a bit of their future to spread democracy and progress to the Third World. Fresh out of college, Elder went to Costa Rica as a Peace Corps volunteer. When he got out two years later, instead of looking for a high-paying job, he became a welfare caseworker in New York City.

There he met Diane, who was working at a hospital with his sister. The tall, dark-haired woman had grown up on Long Island, where her mother was a bank vice-president and her father was in the restaurant and produce business. Diane was active in the antiwar movement. By the time she met Jack, she was organizing protests. Jack came to know Vietnam intimately when, in 1968, he was drafted and sent to work as a hospital lab technician at the Cam Ranh Bay military base.

After Jack's discharge, he and Diane married and moved to San Marcos, Texas, where Jack had taken his Peace Corps training. They managed a picture frame shop and went back to school. Diane commuted to San Antonio, where she studied nursing at San Antonio College. Jack took graduate courses in Central American history at Southwest Texas State University in San Marcos.

In 1974, the couple and their six-month-old son, Jesse, went to El Salvador so Jack could do research. At the urging of an old friend from the Peace Corps, the Elders went to the eastern village of Chirilagua and visited a Catholic lay worker named Rosemary Smith. They only spent one night with Smith, but it was the beginning of a friendship that eventually would change the course of their lives.

In addition to El Salvador, the Elders spent their six-week trip driving through Costa Rica, Guatemala, and Nicaragua. Having lived in Central America before, Jack was familiar with conditions. For Diane, the poverty was shocking. She was also frightened and disturbed by the military presence, especially in Nicaragua, where dictator Anastasio Somoza's National Guard seemed to be everywhere.

Somoza's show of force was meant to intimidate an increasingly restive opposition movement. Nicaraguans expected brutality and corruption from their dictator, but Somoza's efforts to capitalize on a national catastrophe had made them especially bitter. In December 1972, an earthquake had killed more than twenty thousand Nicaraguans and leveled much of Managua, the capital. The dictator managed to avoid the resulting misery. In fact, since the Somoza family controlled much of Nicaragua's construction industry, he had profited handsomely from internationally financed efforts to rebuild the capital. There were also rumors that his National Guard cronies had supplemented their military paychecks with money made by selling international relief supplies. By the end of 1974, the bitterness had spawned a bolder political opposition and a rejuvenated Sandinista National Liberation Front, which renewed its guerrilla war against Somoza.

The Elders kept up with developments in Nicaragua after returning to Texas, although they had plenty in their own lives to keep them busy. The family moved to San Antonio and a two-story home in a quiet middle-class neighborhood a few miles from Fort Sam Houston. Diane found work as a nurse and Jack took a job teaching math at a junior high school. In the evenings, he sometimes waited tables at the prestigious San Antonio Country Club to earn a little money. By then, they had added two more boys — Devin and Richard — to the family. Although Jack worked for the public schools, Diane and he believed that their three sons could get a better education at home. Thus, when the boys reached school age, Diane put her career aside and stayed home to teach them. Jack, meanwhile, got more and more involved with Central American issues.

In 1980, he joined Nicaraguan Assistance, a San Antonio group raising money for the literacy program of Nicaragua's Sandinista government, which had overthrown the Somoza dictatorship the previous year. In addition to fund raising, Elder and the others gave speeches, organized demonstrations, and supplied local reporters with information about Central America. With word of the growing violence in El Salvador and Guatemala, the group broadened its area of interest and changed its name to Latin American Assistance.

Gradually, Jack Elder found himself driven to do more about

the situation to the south. Unlike many of his North American friends, he had lived and worked in Central America, studied its history, and come to know its people. "It's like a plant or something has grown into me," he would say later. "It has roots all through my body."

When Elder heard about Guatemalans and Salvadorans fleeing into Chiapas, he and some friends went to southern Mexico for a week to visit the refugee camps. Occasionally, refugees passing through San Antonio stayed with the Elders. Some would talk late into the night, telling their stories of sons and daughters shot dead in the street, wives and mothers raped and murdered in their homes, husbands and fathers "disappeared."

Meanwhile the news from El Salvador got worse. In late November 1980, five leftist leaders were kidnapped from a meeting at San Salvador high school. Their mutilated bodies were discovered outside the capital a few days later. A week later, four churchwomen from the United States were raped and murdered a few miles from El Salvador's international airport. The brutality of it convinced Elder that there would be no middle road in this struggle.

After hearing stories from his houseguests or reading them in the newspapers and journals, Elder would relay the information to the church and civic groups to which he talked. Some would make a small donation to the cause. Although Elder was glad to accept them, he wanted the North Americans he spoke to do more than scribble out a check. He wanted them to do something, yet, at times, their eyes seemed to glaze over when he spoke. It was as though they thought Elder was weaving some elaborate but impossible nightmare. The frustration began to eat at him.

There were more refugees and more stories. One day, a woman returning from El Salvador brought him some photographs human rights groups had taken of torture victims. It was the sort of evidence Salvadoran families sifted through every day to find out whether their missing relatives had been murdered. For Jack Elder, the black-and-white pictures of hacked and punctured bodies were another reminder that maybe he was not doing all that he could. He and others began finding apartments in San Antonio for the refugees. They drove to the INS detention facility in Los Fresnos on the weekends. There, they bonded out some refugees and helped others complete asylum applications. Some of those who were bonded out ended up staying with the Elder family for a time.

Although sympathetic to the refugees, Diane Elder was still cautious. She did not mind strangers staying at their home if they had papers. But some who came by the house were still hiding from the INS. What if they or the police suddenly appeared one day and arrested her and Jack? Who would take care of the boys?

Then sometime in 1981, a Salvadoran couple came to stay with the Elders. The fighting in their village had taken many lives. They had fled, leaving a baby with its grandparents. That affected Diane Elder more than all the stories she had heard from former political prisoners and torture victims. She could not imagine how any parent could leave a child behind in a war zone. "They must not love their babies like I love mine," she told herself. But as she talked to the family more, Diane Elder learned that, in El Salvador, the security forces watched for parents traveling north with children. Couples heading for the border with their children were probably fleeing the country. In the eyes of the security forces, they were people who were afraid because of some subversive activity with which they had been involved. "Eventually, they got to me," Diane Elder explained. "I realized they were forced to make decisions that I would never have to even consider. And so the refugee reality entered into my own consciousness to the point that I was ready to do more than just go to Latin American Assistance meetings."

To raise money, Latin American Assistance occasionally set up a Mexican food booth at San Antonio festivals and fairs. Diane Elder was selling chalupas at the booth one afternoon when a friend brought a woman by to meet her. Diane recognized the silver-haired stranger from somewhere. After a few minutes of conversation, Diane realized it was Rosemary Smith, the church worker she and Jack had met in El Salvador nearly eight years earlier. At the festival that day, Smith told Diane Elder that she was trying to convince Bishop Fitzpatrick in Brownsville to open a shelter for the Central Americans in the Valley.

A few months after Casa Oscar Romero opened in December 1982, the Elders decided to use Jack's spring break vacation for a camping trip to South Padre Island near Brownsville. They arrived in the midst of a windstorm that made it impossible to pitch a tent. To make matters worse, within a few minutes of their arrival, the family car had to be towed out of the sand. With the evening coming on, Jack and Diane decided that, since they were in the area, it might be a good time to look up Rosemary Smith.

Although she had only been director for a few months, Smith was looking for someone else to run it. Organizing the shelter had worn her down. Running it was too much for one person. During the Elders' two day visit, Smith joked with them about taking over. On the drive back to San Antonio, they discussed it seriously.

Jack was already thinking about leaving the public schools. He found it frustrating to instruct the children of parents who didn't seem to care. He also thought it was somewhat inconsistent for him to teach in the public schools when he and Diane had decided that home schooling was best for their own children. "I just felt I was moving on," he would say later.

Still, before visiting Casa Oscar Romero, the Elders were not certain what to do. They wanted to be involved in social service work, preferably something involving Central American issues, but until Casa Oscar Romero, nothing had presented itself. Even after visiting the Casa, the couple wavered on whether it was the change for which they were looking. They decided that Jack would ask for a leave of absence from school so that they could try it. When the school administration turned down the request, Jack quit and called Rosemary Smith to tell her they would be taking over at the Casa. In August 1983, the Elders loaded their three boys into their aging Plymouth Valiant and drove back to San Benito, where a house trailer and a dozen or so tired and confused refugees were waiting.

A few hundred miles to the north, Stacey Lynn Merkt was in the midst of her own conversion to the refugee cause, one that would eventually lead her to join Jack and Diane Elder in San Benito.

Merkt, twenty nine, had grown up in Pinole, California, a small city just north of San Francisco. She was raised a Methodist and after earning a degree from the University of California at Davis in 1978, Merkt went to live for a year at Koinonia Farms, a Christian community near Americus, Georgia. Later she moved to Bijou House, another religious community in Colorado Springs. There, she worked in the soup kitchen and taught former drunks and derelicts from the city how to farm. Merkt was also involved in the antinuclear movement, at one point joining other demonstrators to block the entrance of the Rocky Flats nuclear plant.

In the early 1980s, Merkt began reading about Central America in the media. She also met a few refugees passing through Colorado. Their stories had a profound impact on her and, in the fall of 1983, she went to Mexico for three months. She spent time in Mexico City, where there was a sizable community of Salvadoran refugees, and in the southern state of Chiapas, where an estimated ninety thousand Guatemalans were living in refugee camps and makeshift settlements. For a time, she worked in a clinic there.

After the experience in Mexico, Merkt returned to the United States determined to help the refugees. She visited Casa Oscar Romero on her way back to Colorado in December 1983. A few weeks later, she returned to San Benito and began teaching Central Americans at the Casa how to speak English. "For me, to start responding to the cry of the people in Central America meant that I had to start living and working and touching these people," she said in an interview with *Sojourners* magazine. "When I went to work at Casa Romero, these people became more than names and numbers and faces and events. They became María and José, and I put living flesh onto statistics."

Two of the refugees she came to know at Casa Romero were Mauricio Valle, twenty-three, and Brenda Sánchez-Galán, nineteen. Both Salvadorans belonged to the Resurrection Lutheran Church in San Salvador. Both had also worked for the church's Faith and Hope Refugee Camp, Valle as a driver and Sánchez-

Galán as a nurse. The two young Salvadorans had had friends and neighbors murdered by the security forces, but it was their work at Faith and Hope that ultimately forced them to flee El Salvador.

Refugee camp workers had become frequent targets of the security forces and the death squads, who contended that the camps were havens for guerrilla sympathizers. Faith and Hope, which aided more than six hundred refugees who had fled zones in conflict in northern El Salvador, had been hit particularly hard. During 1983, several of its workers were arrested or kidnapped. In April, the National Police arrested the camp's medical director, Dr. Angel Ibarra, and the Rev. Medardo Gómez, pastor of the Resurrection church and president of the Lutheran church in El Salvador. Although Gómez was released within a few days, Ibarra was detained and tortured until October.

Brenda Sánchez-Galán and her baby daughter fled two months later, following the rape and murder of a pregnant friend. Mauricio Valle, who had been questioned several times about his work at the camp and also threatened with death, left at the same time. They made their way to Casa Romero, hoping to travel on to San Antonio to see the Rev. Dan Long, a Lutheran minister who had worked closely with Salvadoran Lutherans.

At Casa Romero, Merkt befriended the two Salvadorans and offered to help them get to San Antonio. They could apply for political asylum at the district INS office there. The district office in nearby Harlingen was closer, but Salvadorans and Guatemalans who applied there were rarely granted asylum by the district director. Merkt had heard that some were detained after filing their applications.

Plans were made to take the Salvadorans north on the morning of February 17, 1984. Merkt and the refugees were to be joined by Sister Diane Muhlenkamp, thirty-six, of Fort Wayne, Indiana, who had come to the Casa to study the refugee situation. Also riding with them would be Jack Fischer, a reporter from the *Dallas Times-Herald*. Fischer had covered the movement's growth in Dallas, where a handful of churches had declared sanctuary. He had gone to the Valley to write a story about the underground railroad.

They left before dawn, taking a circuitous route that took them far to the west before they turned north toward San Antonio. They were on a deserted stretch of rural road near Hebbronville, Texas, when the Border Patrol flagged them down. Sánchez-Galán and Valle were detained as witnesses against the three U.S. citizens, all of whom were arrested on smuggling charges.

Justice Department officials in Washington declined to prosecute Fischer. Federal prosecutors in Texas worked out a plea bargain agreement with Sister Muhlenkamp whereby she would not be prosecuted in return for becoming a government witness. That left Stacey Lynn Merkt as the first member of the sanctuary movement to go on trial for working with the refugees. Within weeks, however, it became clear she would not be the last.

Jack and Diane Elder had talked about the possibility of arrest long before they came to San Benito. With three young sons and a fourth child on the way, neither was anxious to spend time in jail. "Nobody wants to be an unnecessary martyr," Jack had told a reporter a few weeks before moving to the Valley. But at that point arrest for working at the Casa seemed unlikely. It had been operating for months. News media across Texas had done stories about it. The INS knew it was there. In fact, Border Patrolmen sometimes took refugees they had caught to the Casa.

In their interviews with reporters, INS officials had said they had no plans to single the sanctuary movement out for prosecution, although if a driver for the underground railroad fell into their surveillance net, he or she would be arrested. Apparently, that had been Stacey Merkt's misfortune.

Even after his coworker's arrest, Elder continued transporting refugees from the Casa to the bus stations and airports. Transporting illegal aliens was part of life in the Rio Grande Valley. Every day, local farmers drove their undocumented workers into the fields and wealthy Anglo women picked their Mexican maids up at the border and took them to their homes to work. Except for smugglers moving large numbers of people, transporting within the Valley was usually not a problem. The people who ran into trouble with the INS were those who tried to take undocumented aliens north.

On the night of March 12, 1983, three Salvadorans asked Elder to take them to the bus station in nearby Harlingen. Elder warned the Salvadorans that, without papers, they would be easy prey for the Border Patrol agents who watched the local airports and bus stations. But the refugees insisted and Elder finally agreed to take them.

Six days later, the Elders and Casa Oscar Romero were the subject of a cover story in the Sunday magazine of the *San Antonio Light,* one of the largest-circulation newspapers in South Texas. *Light* writer Dan Freedman had done his reporting for the piece in February, just a week before Stacey Merkt's arrest. While several other stories had been written about the Casa, the sanctuary movement, and the underground railroad, the prominently displayed *Light* piece strongly implied that the three were linked.

One month after taking the three refugees to Harlingen, the Elders got a call from a friend in Laredo. He told them he was working with three Salvadorans who were being held in the county jail there as witnesses for a federal grand jury in Brownsville. They had been arrested at the Harlingen bus station and were being questioned about the man who had taken them there. Their names were Valentín Cruz, Tránsito Fuentes, and Epífano Canales. Did Elder know them?

Jack and Diane remembered the unusual first names. They looked in the notebook they used to keep track of the refugees who passed through the Casa. The names were recorded there. They were the men Jack had taken to Harlingen. The Elders had several weeks to think about what the grand jury and the government would do. They got their answer when the federal marshals came to arrest Jack and impound the family's car.

Stacey Merkt's trial opened the first week in May in a federal courtroom in Brownsville, an impoverished city on the southern tip of the United States. Brownsville was the first bit of the United States many Central Americans saw when they crossed the Rio Grande. It also became the first city in which one of the sanctuary workers who helped them faced a jury.

Merkt pleaded not guilty to the smuggling charges, which carried a maximum sentence of fifteen years in prison and a $9,000 fine. Her attorney was Daniel Sheehan, a former Jesuit priest, who had been one of the attorneys in the Karen Silkwood case. In an emotional opening statement before the jury, Sheehan talked about the land of torture and murder that the two refugees had fled. He compared the Salvadorans to Mary and Joseph, who fled their homeland with the young Jesus after Herod threatened to kill all the babies. Sheehan said his client had no specific intention to violate federal law but was attempting to get the Salvadorans to San Antonio, where they planned to file for political asylum.

Assistant U.S. Attorney Robert Guerra portrayed it less dramatically. Stacey Merkt had tried to help some illegal aliens avoid apprehension by the Border Patrol. It was a black-and-white case of smuggling.

Brenda Sánchez-Galán and Mauricio Valle, the two Salvadorans Merkt was accused of transporting, were jailed for a weekend when they refused to testify for the prosecution. U.S. District Judge Filemón Vela released them after they agreed to appear as defense witnesses. Sánchez-Galán tearfully told the jury about an incident in which she and some other bus passengers were forced to take cover in a San Salvador parking garage after the vehicle they were riding in was caught in a crossfire. Some young men in the group tried to protect the others, but they were shot down when security forces opened fire from the garage door.

The following day, Merkt told the jury she had agreed to aid the refugees because she believed that if they were returned to El Salvador, they would be murdered. Merkt testified that she was taking them to the INS office in San Antonio because she had been told the INS district director in Harlingen arrested Salvadorans who applied for asylum.

The members of the jury were unimpressed. After seventeen hours of deliberation, they found Merkt guilty. A few weeks later, she stood before Judge Vela again for sentencing. She told him that her religious beliefs had led her to work on behalf of the poor and the oppressed:

> We've lost sight of the fact that when our sister or

brother anywhere hurts, we hurt. I see that and I have
to respond. I cannot not respond.

If we participate in a demonstration here it's not likely we'll be shot. In El Salvador, it is likely. If we teach
people to read, we aren't called subversive and Communist and then disappear. In El Salvador, it is likely.
For there is not justice. We've already seen forty thousand deaths there, mostly all civilians killed by government forces. The Reagan Administration continues
to support that government — the government that cre-
ates the refugees.

I'm no celebrity. I'm not a martyr. And I'm no felon.
I am a woman with a heart and mind. My faith commitment connects me to people and to justice.

Judge Vela told Merkt that, although he believed her to be a
woman of "high intentions and high ideals," breaking the law
was not the way to achieve them. He then sentenced her to two
years probation, adding that if she ever appeared before him
again he would put her in prison.

Jack Elder was still working at Casa Romero and waiting for
his trial to begin. If Merkt's conviction frightened him, he gave
no sign of it. If anything, he was cutting a higher profile than
ever. At a September news conference on Capitol Hill, Elder told
reporters he planned to use the trial to the advantage of the refugees. "We are unrepentent. We are unbowed," he said. "We
intend to continue helping refugees who come here from El Salvador, and through this forum [the trial] bring focus upon what
is going on in El Salvador."

Beside Elder that day were two men who had already provided
depositions for his defense. As U.S. ambassador to El Salvador
during the Carter years, Robert White had frequently critized
human rights abuses in that country, incurring the wrath of both
right-wing militarists and the new Reagan administration, which
fired him within days of taking office. Also with Elder was Bill
Ford, brother of one of four American churchwomen slain outside
San Salvador in December 1980. Both were well known to jour-

nalists and legislators who followed Salvadoran issues. Their involvement was also indicative of the sort of attention Elder
wanted for his trial. Instead of a jury simply deciding whether he
had driven a few aliens through the Valley, Elder wanted the
nation to judge whether its policy toward the refugees was just.

But before the depositions from White, Ford, and more than
two dozen others could be used in court, the federal government
fattened the stack of charges against Elder. December 4, 1984,
was the fourth anniversary of the day Robert White watched as
the mutilated bodies of Bill Ford's sister and three other American
churchwomen were pulled from roadside graves in rural El Salvador. It was also the day that a federal grand jury in Brownsville
indicted both Stacey Merkt and Jack Elder on additional counts
of smuggling Salvadorans trying to flee such brutality.

But even as defense attorneys for Elder and Merkt prepared to
meet the newest charges, the INS and federal prosecutors were
putting the finishing touches on the biggest challenge yet to the
sanctuary movement. This time, the battleground would be Arizona. This time the evidence would not be supplied by refugees
nabbed at a Border Patrol checkpoint but by government informants who had infiltrated the movement.

10

A Grandfatherly Informant

On Thursdays, Father Rámon Dagoberto Quiñones usually said mass at the federal penitentiary in Nogales, a small border town in the Mexican state of Sonora. With his square jaw, broad nose, and dark, swept-back hair, the forty-seven-year-old priest was an institution in Nogales. So was his white stucco church, the Sanctuary of Our Lady of Guadalupe, built in a hilly residential neighborhood about a mile from the chain link fence that marked the end of the Third World and the beginning of the wealthiest nation on earth. The United States was a beacon that drew Latin Americans through Nogales. Some crossed the fence and never returned. Others were caught by the U.S. Border Patrol and quickly pushed back.

They were among the people Father Quiñones met at the prison. The priest heard the inmates' confessions and gave them communion. He also acted as their advocate on matters as temporal as disposal of the sewage that sometimes backed up into their cells. Some of the prisoners the priest visited were common criminals. Others were Central Americans who had been caught on their way to Arizona or California. The Mexican government's Benjamin Hill roadblock on the highway to Hermosillo always kept the prison well stocked with refugees. The Central Americans were jailed in Nogales until the Mexican government got around to shipping them back to Guatemala, El Salvador, or other countries.

When they left, many of the deportees took word of Father Quiñones's kindness with them. The next time they or their

friends tried to make it to the United States, they again headed
for Nogales, where they knew help could be found. Since the early
1980s, Quiñones church had served as a shelter for Salvadorans
and Guatemalans who managed either to elude Mexican authorities or to bribe their way past them. Thanks to North Americans
in the sanctuary movement, it had also become known as a place
where at least some of the refugees could make contact with people who would help them cross the border.

Jim Corbett met Father Quiñones soon after he began smuggling refugees out of Nogales in 1981. In the months that followed, the Quaker rancher posed as a Catholic priest and visited
the prison with Quiñones every Thursday. While the real clergyman said mass for the Mexican prisoners, "Padre Jaime" interviewed the Central Americans about where they had come from
and what they had seen. He took messages to pass on to their relatives and distributed food and clothing. Corbett also told them
about North Americans who were willing to help them get past
the U.S. Border Patrol if they tried the journey again. Word of
this also rippled through the refugee grapevine.

At the same time he was meeting deportees at the prison, Corbett was leading other refugees through the chain link border
fence, across the desert, and on to Tucson. By mid-1982, he was
taking reporters and camera crews with him on a regular basis.
Although the publicity spread the word about the refugees' plight,
it also made it more difficult for Corbett to work unrecognized in
Nogales, Mexico, or Tucson, Arizona, for that matter.

As the media attention grew more intense, Corbett made
fewer trips to the prison. Of course, by then the Mexican jailers
had gotten used to seeing North Americans arrive with Father
Quiñones every Thursday. The sanctuary workers going in place
of Corbett no longer bothered to pose as priests or nuns. Among
them was a Californian named Phil Conger.

Conger, a thin, soft-spoken man with a wispy moustache, was
the son of two Methodist missionaries who had settled in San
Diego after working in Peru and Bolivia during the 1950s. They
became teachers, but their religious commitment lived on in their
son. As a boy, Phil had spent nearly a year traveling with his
parents through Latin America. In San Diego, he became presi-

dent of the youth group at the family's church and later youth director at the church's summer camp. After earning a degree in Spanish from San Diego State, Conger signed up for a church volunteer program that sent him to Tucson for two years to work for a Methodist organization that served low-income people and Hispanics.

Conger arrived in August 1980. At the time, Tucson churches were still caring for Salvadorans who had survived the desert tragedy outside Ajo. Having grown up with an interest in Latin America, Conger began attending the Thursday afternoon prayer vigils at the Tucson federal building and various Central American programs at the nearby University of Arizona. Within a year, he was joining Corbett, John Fife, and others on their trips to California to bond Central Americans out of the INS detention center at El Centro.

As the months passed, Conger met more refugees, heard their stories, and moved slowly toward a greater commitment to helping them. In June 1982, he became project director of the Tucson Ecumenical Council's Task Force for Central America. Made up of sixty-five Tucson-area churches, the TEC had set up the task force after Ajo to provide refugees with social services, to lobby in their behalf, and to educate the Tucson community about Central American issues. Although the TEC had issued a statement in support of Southside Presbyterian's sanctuary declaration, its members had decided not to become directly involved. Unofficially, however, some of the people connected with the TEC were also active in sanctuary work.

Conger soon began accompanying Corbett on his trips to Nogales, where he met sanctuary contacts on both sides of the border. In addition to Father Quiñones in Mexico, there was María del Socorro Pardo de Aguilar, a lay worker at the priest's church. The fifty-six-year-old widow visited the prison and had opened her home to Mexicans and Central Americans on their way to the United States. On the Arizona side, Conger got acquainted with Father Tony Clark, youth director at the Sacred Heart Catholic Church and founder of a home for delinquent boys. He also met Mary K. Doan Espinoza, the daughter of a former Nogales mayor. She was working with Father Clark at

Sacred Heart. Clark and Espinoza provided food and shelter to refugees once they made it through the border fence. Like Father Quiñones, they kept in touch with the sanctuary movement's underground railroad.

Conger did not begin running the Border Patrol roadblocks immediately, but after spending so much time with Corbett and other sanctuary sympathizers, it was not a giant step when he finally made it. Corbett, Conger, and some other church workers had driven a TEC car to Nogales one Thursday afternoon for the regular prison visit. Before going back, they learned that a Salvadoran who had already made it through the border fence needed to get to Tucson.

If they did not take the Salvadoran to Tucson with them, another underground railroad driver would have to come back to Nogales later to pick him up. Corbett asked his companions what they wanted to do. The Salvadoran returned to Tucson in their car. Conger made the border runs more and more. At first, the sanctuary work was done on his own time, but by early 1983, it had become part of his job description at the TEC. In addition to raising money for bonds and legal fees, Conger helped the refugees find jobs, housing, and medical assistance in Tucson. He also spoke to area churches about the sanctuary movement.

The government was still complaining that the movement was using religion as a pretext for reaching its political goals, but Conger had already worked through that argument for himself. "My understanding of my faith is that I am called to work in this world to make a better world," he would say later. "That means working against institutions or people or traditions that tend to devalue human life or human dignity. In the Old Testament, that meant decrying poor treatment of the poor, the orphans and the widows. It meant crying out against the corruption of government officials in Jesus' time. It means that we work in any way we can to change our world. That means our right to vote, that means lobbying congressmen and senators, demonstrations and rallies, educational forums—all the normal ways we have of impacting and changing our society."

For Conger, it also meant civil disobedience. By the end of 1983, he and the other sanctuary drivers had gained enough experience to know which roads the Border Patrol watched, what times the surveillance was heaviest, and even when the shifts changed. Bringing back refugees after the Thursday trips to Nogales became a regular part of the routine for Conger and other prison visitors.

In early 1984, Katherine Flaherty, thirty-two, came to Tucson to help. After earning a master's degree in rehabilitation counseling from George Washington University in 1977, Flaherty had gone to El Salvador as a Peace Corps volunteer. Two years later, she returned to Washington, D.C., to found the Religious Task Force on El Salvador. Before going to Tucson, Flaherty had been a leader of sanctuary efforts in the Washington, D.C., area.

She made her first trip to Nogales with Phil Conger on the morning of March 7, 1984. It was a Wednesday. Father Quiñones had decided to visit the prison one day early so that he could celebrate Ash Wednesday with the prisoners. Conger and Flaherty drove to the border in an old Ford station wagon owned by Southside Presbyterian Church. Before leaving, he threw a knapsack containing all of his work papers into the back of the car.

After visiting the prison, Conger was asked to take four Salvadorans back to Tucson. Among them was Oscar Antonio Andrade, a twenty-four-year-old student activist who had already been deported once from the United States. María Camero Colocho, a catechist from La Libertad, had worked with the four American churchwomen who had been murdered by Salvadoran National Guardsmen in December 1980. The catechist's two younger sisters were traveling with her.

Conger called Tucson and asked a friend to come to Nogales to serve as the "lead" driver. He would leave a few minutes ahead of Conger's car to scout the highway for the Border Patrol roadblocks. By the time the lead driver got to Nogales, it was getting late. Knowing that the Border Patrol was more likely to stop a car at night, Conger considered calling the run off, but that would only mean making another drive to the border the following day.

It was after 10:30 P.M. by the time Conger, Flaherty, and their four Salvadoran passengers headed north on U.S. Highway 82. As they drove, Conger taught Flaherty some of the finer points of driving for the underground railroad. Approaching the entrance to the Nogales airport, Conger pointed toward a side road and noted that sometimes the Border Patrol parked at just such a spot and watched for cars that might be smuggling aliens.

At that second, a pair of headlights flashed from the side road. Conger tapped his brakes, but kept going. He watched in the rearview mirror as a Border Patrol vehicle pulled onto the highway and began following them.

It had been a slow day for agents Herman Baca and Charles Chase, both eight-year veterans of the Border Patrol. By the time Conger's car drove past them, they had stopped only one suspicious vehicle in more than six hours of watching the same stretch of highway. When they hit the Conger station wagon with their lights, Baca and Chase noticed that it was a large, older car, the sort smugglers used. The station wagon also seemed to be riding low in back, although there was no luggage visible in the windows. They decided to pull the car over.

The agents walked up to the station wagon and shone their flashlights onto the Salvadorans riding in back. Conger asked what the trouble was, but he already knew.

Back at the Border Patrol office in Nogales, Chase soon learned that they had stumbled upon more than another case of smuggling. Looking through Conger's backpack, they found a treasure chest of information about the sanctuary movement. Conger's appointment books for 1983 and 1984 included the names of sanctuary sympathizers he had met with for the previous year and a half. His address book had the names and numbers of refugees and sanctuary workers from Tucson to Juneau, Alaska, as well as notes about meetings. There were also letters from people whose relatives needed to be smuggled out of Nogales and a sheet labeled "pre-crossing counseling," which advised sanctuary workers to give refugees crossing the border fake names to use and also to make certain all identifying labels had been removed from their clothing.

The Salvadorans were detained. Conger and Flaherty were released, but not before Border Patrol agents had questioned them and made copies of everything in Conger's knapsack.

It was the second piece of substantial intelligence on the sanctuary movement that the INS had obtained in less than a month. Following a routine traffic stop three weeks earlier, Tucson police had questioned a man claiming to be from southern Mexico. He was driving a car belonging to an Arizona woman. In it the police had found a number of papers relating to the sanctuary movement. Among them was a list of names and phone numbers, including those of Jim Corbett and Phil Conger. Also in the car was a set of instructions on how a refugee was to travel from Tapachula to Oaxaca, Mexico. The information was passed on to INS intelligence agents.

On March 23, Tucson INS chief William Johnston told a meeting of the Pima County (Tucson) Republican Women that the sanctuary movement had not generated a great deal of excitement within immigration circles. "If they happen to get caught, our officers will treat them just like everybody else," the *Arizona Daily Star* reported him as saying. "But at this time, we have no specific plans for them."

Johnston and his superiors must not have been in close contact, for whereas the INS may not have decided on a "specific" plan, it was certainly well on the way to developing one for the movement, which had just added its one-hundredth church.

INS investigators in Arizona had been keeping the movement under surveillance since the first press conference at Southside Presbyterian Church in March 1982. There were INS undercover agents there and press reports were monitored closely in the months that followed.

On June 30, 1983, investigator James Rayburn of the Phoenix INS office sent his superiors a memo entitled, "El Salvadorian Underground Railroad." In it, Rayburn said both John Fife and Jim Corbett claimed to be transporting illegal aliens. "These claims are well orchestrated to the news media," he wrote. Rayburn added that the movement's practice was to use the same aliens for different news stories.

The agent also noted that three months earlier, he had monitored a public debate between John Fife and an INS official. As a result of what he had heard at the debate, Rayburn wrote that "it is now clear that they plan to force U.S. Immigration to take them to court on either harboring charges or transportation

charges. The . . . movement will then use the trial as their stage
to challenge both U.S. policy on Central America and [INS]
policy."

Rayburn's memo also indicated that INS surveillance of
the sanctuary movement went beyond agents reading newspapers and monitoring public debates. Rayburn said the INS
had learned through an informant that, in addition to Father
Quiñones's church in Nogales, Sonora, the sanctuary movement
had made contact with refugees in Hermosillo at a Catholic
church, a hotel, and the local Red Cross office. The information
came from Hermosillo smugglers who complained that the sanctuary movement was cutting into their business.

Rayburn, who had been with the INS for fourteen years, concluded that the movement was transporting "a very low number"
of aliens, but the investigation continued. A week after the first
memo, Rayburn wrote a second stating that INS informants had
taken photographs and recorded speeches at a rally at a Presbyterian church in Phoenix. He also noted that agents had finally
gotten a license number and home address for Jim Corbett. An
agent was to check Corbett's home to see about the possibilities
of further surveillance.

In January 1984, Rayburn got a new boss. Robert "Scott"
Coffin had been with the INS for sixteen years before being appointed supervisor of the Phoenix office's antismuggling investigation unit. Within two months of his arrival in Arizona, he got
a call from INS western regional headquarters in San Pedro,
California. The call was a result of an earlier meeting between
Mark Kevin Reed, assistant regional commissioner for antismuggling, and Harold Ezell, the INS commissioner for the
western region. The sanctuary movement had been getting a lot
of publicity, much of it sympathetic. That worried INS officials
in Washington and San Pedro. Ezell wanted to know what sort
of investigation Coffin had going.

Coffin turned to Rayburn, who told him that at one time the
Phoenix INS office had been gathering intelligence on the sanctuary movement, but other investigations seemed to get higher
priority. Rayburn told Coffin that if the INS finally wanted to
concentrate on the sanctuary movement, he knew someone who

could get close to the people involved.

Before Rayburn could actually put his plan into action, Phil Conger's arrest provided the INS with new intelligence. Charles Chase, the Border Patrol agent who had stopped Conger, was sent to regional INS headquarters in San Pedro to discuss the arrest with officials there.

Conger's arrest provided the INS with a plethora of new intelligence — dates, names, addresses, phone numbers. INS officials decided that what had once seemed like an insignificant movement had grown too large to ignore. The longer they waited, the more difficult shutting it down would be. By the end of March, a decision had been made to infiltrate the church-based movement. For help, the INS investigators turned to two Mexican nationals with firsthand knowledge of the smuggling game.

Just four days after the Tucson INS chief had said that there were no specific plans for the sanctuary movement, a stranger visited Father Quiñones at his church in Nogales, Sonora. Jesús Cruz, fifty-seven, was a portly, balding man with big ears, a long nose, and salt-and-pepper hair. Cruz arrived early enough that morning to have breakfast. As they ate, Cruz told the priest he was a part-time roofer from Phoenix who had, in the past, helped illegal aliens cross the border. He said he was sympathetic to the plight of the Central Americans and after hearing about the sanctuary movement, had decided he wanted to help.

Sanctuary workers in Arizona and Sonora were on the watch for possible infiltration, but Cruz, an affable, grandfatherly type who always wore a crucifix, seemed harmless. Beyond that, he appeared to be genuinely interested in the refugees. Cruz continued to visit Quiñones and offer his services. By mid-April, he was joining the priest on his prison visits. One day when he arrived, his old brown pickup was loaded with oranges, tangerines, and grapefruit for the prisoners.

About three weeks after first appearing in Nogales, Cruz asked to meet Philip Conger. He told Father Quiñones he was interested in getting to know a man who was doing so much for the refugees. The priest introduced the two men during one of

Conger's Thursday visits.

The Tucson sanctuary organizer was mildly suspicious. He called friends in Phoenix to check on a church program Cruz claimed to have worked with years earlier. While no one remembered Jesús Cruz, the program had existed at one time. The information allayed Conger's concerns enough that he continued to meet with Cruz. The new volunteer accompanied Quiñones to the prison, helped Conger take refugees to the border fence, and visited them at safe houses on the Arizona side. He also began attending sanctuary meetings at Southside Presbyterian. With volunteers sometimes in short supply, Cruz was eventually allowed to transport refugees to Tucson, Phoenix, Los Angeles, and Seattle.

Cruz kept close track of his work for the movement. He jotted names, places, and meetings down in a small notebook. He also used a body bug to tape dozens of conversations with Conger, John Fife, and others. None of the other sanctuary volunteers went to such lengths to document their work with the movement, but that is what the INS was paying Cruz to do.

Actually, only one element of the story Cruz had told Quiñones and others was true: he was an experienced smuggler of aliens. In September 1978, Cruz began driving undocumented workers from Phoenix to Bonita Springs, Florida. He earned about $6,000 over the next year, transporting up to two dozen Mexicans per trip. The endeavor ended only after Cruz learned that the INS was closing in on him. He turned himself in to federal investigators. Instead of being prosecuted, Cruz was pleasantly surprised to learn that his smuggling skills were in demand on the other side of the law. Beginning in 1980, he became an informant for the INS. Over the next few years, he worked on cases in Florida, Idaho, Oregon, and West Virginia. His primary INS contact was James Rayburn, the same man who had begun investigating the sanctuary movement.

By 1984, Rayburn had decided that Jesús Cruz was the man to infiltrate the movement. In a March memo to an INS board that had to approve such undercover operations, Rayburn said Cruz would "claim to be a non-profit smuggler motivated by a strong desire to help the cause." Cruz, he added, "has extensive experience in dealing with illegal aliens. . . . His appearance and age make him highly acceptable and believable in the cover he will present to the alleged principal subjects."

The same memo outlined the goals for "Operation Sojourner," as the investigation was called. In addition to providing the INS with information about routes, safe houses, drivers, and vehicles, the investigation would tell them what "class" of refugees were being aided by the sanctuary movement and what sort of "coaching" they were getting on how to cross the border. Such goals might have fit any INS investigation, but what Rayburn proposed went beyond breaking up a smuggling ring. In his memo, he also wrote of determining the "true purpose" of the movement and whether it constituted a threat to the sovereignty of the United States. Rayburn added that the intelligence gathered might help the INS "neutralize" the publicity the sanctuary movement had been receiving.

After being discussed by INS officials in Washington, Rayburn's first application was turned down for lack of details. His second was approved on May 4. By then, Cruz had already made his first contact with Father Quiñones. Three days later, he began taping telephone conversations with Conger and others.

Cruz was not the only informer the INS paid to infiltrate the movement. He was joined by his roommate, Salomón Graham Delgado, a thirty-two-year-old Mexican who had also been working with the INS since 1979. Graham, also known as Henry Graham and Henry Perea Smith, was the informant who had provided Rayburn with the information from professional smugglers in Hermosillo one year earlier. Like Cruz, Graham knew how to speak their language.

He had been arrested for illegal entry into the United States four times between 1970 and 1978. In 1974, he had been charged with transporting illegal aliens in Tucson. He received a suspended sentence after pleading guilty to a lesser charge. Two years later, he was arrested on similar charges in Yuma, Arizona. He was convicted and spent three and a half months in prison.

Younger and more sullen than his partner, Graham did not seem to the sanctuary workers to be the sort of man who would sacrifice his time for humanitarian pursuits. But Cruz introduced

Graham as his nephew and business partner, and the sanctuary
workers were willing to believe him. The Rev. John Fife allowed
the two men to attend the sanctuary meetings at his church.
"I thought Jesús was on a rehabilitation project with his ne'er-
do-well nephew," Fife said later. "I figured, well, we're in
the business of converting people. Maybe even Salomón can be
redeemed."

Still, sanctuary workers in Arizona had good reason to suspect
that the days of government tolerance were dwindling. In May,
a jury in Brownsville, Texas convicted sanctuary worker Stacey
Merkt of three counts of transporting illegal aliens stemming from
her arrest at a Border Patrol roadblock three months earlier.
Although Merkt was not given a prison sentence, it was a clear
signal that humanitarian goals would not exempt the sanctuary
workers from prosecution and conviction.

In the weeks following his March 1984 arrest outside Nogales,
no charges were filed against Philip Conger. But within days of
Merkt's conviction in Texas, a federal grand jury in Arizona indicted Conger on four counts of transporting illegal aliens.

Also following Merkt's conviction, INS commisioner Alan
Nelson sent a letter of congratulations to Daniel Hedges, U.S. attorney for southern Texas. The letter was also a response to
Hedges's request for guidance on how to handle sanctuary cases
in the future.

Nelson advised Hedges to continue "routine prosecution" of all
violators of the smuggling, transporting, and harboring statutes
if they were apprehended in the normal course of business.
Members of the sanctuary movement would not get any "special
exemption" from prosecution. "Conversely, there has not been
nor will there be special targeting of such individuals or groups
for prosecution," added the commissioner, who was apparently
unaware that his own people were well along in just such an investigation in Arizona.

In the same letter—later sent to other federal prosecutors—
Nelson outlined the government's "general policy positions" re-
garding the movement. That position amounted to a guide to
undermining the movement's legitimacy via the press.

Nelson suggested that U.S. attorneys and INS officials point out to reporters that, although members of the movement could criticize and lobby against immigration policy, they had no right to take the law into their own hands. Federal officials might also suggest that the movement workers were diverting time and resources from "legitimate refugees" and risking substantial fines and jail sentences. Further, they did not have the support they claimed to, Nelson argued.

They enjoyed enough support, however, for Nelson to suggest ways of tearing the movement apart. "Since foreign policy is the principal motivation of proponents of the movement," the commissioner wrote in the same memo, "their alleged 'humanitarian' motives must be questioned." He suggested doing that by pointing out the movement did not encourage "democratic principles" in El Salvador, Nicaragua, and elsewhere. The INS commissioner also noted that the movement did not promote sanctuary for Nicaraguans. (This is an interesting point. Through the CIA, the Reagan administration had been promoting "democratic principles" in Nicaragua by mining that nation's harbors, publishing murder manuals, and funneling arms to a guerrilla army led by remnants of the Anastasio Somoza's National Guard. Congress eventually decided to withhold funding for such activities, but it continued thanks to organizations funded by the religious right, various mercenary groups and, as would become clear in 1986, operatives within the White House. At the same time the administration was turning up the pressure on church groups bringing refugees into this country, it had showed no interest in prosecuting possible violations of the Neutrality Act by *contra* supporters.)

And so while some federal officials publicly portrayed the movement as a minor nuisance, in secret they were developing strategies to cripple it. The government assigned a special assistant U.S. attorney named Donald Reno to prosecute Conger. Earlier in his legal career, Reno had earned his living defending antiwar protestors and bookshop owners accused of selling pornography. Now the slim and debonair attorney represented the government in smuggling cases.

Conger chose a skilled but unlikely pair of lawyers to defend him. The clean-cut son of an FBI agent, Bates Butler III had spent several years in the local district attorney's office. Later, he prosecuted smugglers, mobsters, and murderers as a U.S. attorney in Arizona. After returning to private practice, Butler had taken an interest in the sanctuary movement when his church began debating the issue. Butler's cocounsel in the Conger case was Robert Hirsch, a lanky criminal defense attorney known for his aggressive and abrasive tactics in the courtroom. The attorney for several reputed organized crime figures, Hirsch had been Butler's opponent in the past. Now the two attorneys pooled their talents to defend Conger.

Although he admitted to transporting the refugees on the night of his arrest, Conger pleaded not guilty to the charges. He planned to use his trial as a forum to challenge the U.S. immigration policy toward the Central American refugees, but the case never got that far.

The Border Patrolmen who arrested Conger had said that one of the reasons they stopped the station wagon was that it appeared to be sagging in the rear, perhaps a sign that the driver was hauling hidden cargo. In July, U.S. District Judge Alfredo Márquez moved the proceedings into the parking lot outside the courthouse. There, using a yardstick, he found that loading six people into the station wagon only caused the car's rear bumper to sag about 2.5 inches. As a result, Judge Márquez ruled that the Border Patrol had no probable cause to stop Conger.

After Márquez suppressed all the evidence gathered in the stop, Reno decided to drop the charges. But the prosecutor was clearly not giving up on the sanctuary movement. "Sooner or later, they will run afoul," he told reporters. "We may be back someday."

Even as Tucson sanctuary workers were celebrating the technical victory, infiltrators were burrowing deeper all around them. That summer, Cruz introduced two new "volunteers" into the movement. John Powers and Lou L'Beau presented themselves as machinery salesmen who had stopped to help Cruz after his truck broke down on the highway. After meeting the refugees Cruz was hauling that day, Powers and L'Beau claimed, they had been moved to spend their free time helping the sanctuary movement. In truth, Powers and L'Beau were John Nixon and Lee Morgan, two undercover INS investigators.

John Fife did not trust Powers and L'Beau, but neither did he make any move to exclude them from sanctuary work. "We have never thrown anybody out just because we had suspicions," he would say later. "If we start that, we're going to be very paranoid people and we're not going to be the church anymore, we're going to be a conspiracy."

As the summer drew to a close, Jesús Cruz was so confident about his cover that he began contacting local reporters. In August, *Arizona* (Tucson) *Daily Star* reporter Carmen Duarte wrote a series describing one Guatemalan woman's journey from Mexico City to Tucson via the underground railroad. After the stories were published, Cruz phoned the *Daily Star* several times to enquire about the woman's whereabouts. He claimed to represent some Phoenix people who were interested in helping her.

In addition to meetings of the Tucson Ecumenical Council's Central American Task Force, Cruz was also attending—and sometimes taping—Sunday night Bible studies at Alzona Lutheran Church, a sanctuary outpost in Phoenix. The meetings, led by the Rev. Jim Oines, were a gathering point for Central Americans in the Phoenix area. The church distributed donated food on Sunday nights. The refugees also prayed, sang hymns, and discussed how various chapters in the Bible related to their exodus from Central America.

From the beginning of the sanctuary movement, INS officials had said repeatedly that they did not plan to raid churches to arrest refugees, but by the fall of 1984, they had a paid infiltrator attending and taping church services in Phoenix. Cruz also gave many refugees rides to the Sunday meetings at Alzona. He then turned their addresses, along with notes from the meetings, over to Rayburn.

Sanctuary workers in Tucson were growing more suspicious of Cruz and the three volunteers he had brought into the movement. They began hearing reports that, while transporting the refugees, Cruz and the others were quizzing them about who they were, where they had come from, and where they were going. In September, leaders of the movement in Tucson decided that, although they did not want to totally exclude anyone from the movement, they would stop discussing the details of the border crossing when Cruz or the others were present. They would also try to keep him from having direct contact with the refugees.

But it was too late, Cruz's tapes and notes had already provided the INS with enough names, addresses, and dates to launch a full-scale roundup of refugees and supporters. Still, the investigation continued.

In Los Angeles, undercover INS investigator Guadalupe Ochoa was monitoring meetings of Central American refugees and rallies organized by the sanctuary movement. On September 30, she attended the First Unitarian Church in Los Angeles, which had decided to accept a refugee family into sanctuary. Among the guest speakers that day was the Rev. Jesse Jackson, civil rights leader, former presidential candidate, and leader of Operation Push, headquartered in Chicago. In a memo to regional INS headquarters in San Pedro, Ochoa reported that Jackson announced that all Operation Push offices were opening their doors to the refugees. "He concluded his speech with the regular Anti-Reagan comments much to the delight of the crowd," Ochoa reported.

The INS did not limit its monitoring activities to meetings and rallies. That October, Jesús Cruz even wore a body bug to Conger's wedding to another sanctuary worker, Ellen Willis (both subsequently used the last name Willis-Conger).

The Reagan administration was taking an intense interest in Operation Sojourner. Normally, the local INS offices decided on whether to prosecute smuggling cases, but in late 1984, Rayburn was called to Washington to review his investigation with INS commissioner Alan C. Nelson, special federal prosecutor Donald Reno, and other officials. As the investigation continued, Rayburn received so many calls from INS officials that he complained to his immediate superiors that proper channels of communication were not being observed.

The first signs of the crackdown came from Texas. On December 4, a federal grand jury in Brownsville handed down an eight-count indictment against Stacey Merkt and Jack Elder. Elder, who had not yet been tried on the charges filed against him the previous April, was accused of driving two Salvadorans from Brownsville to Casa Oscar Romero in San Benito. Merkt was charged with driving those same two refugees on to McAllen.

In a statement to reporters, Elder made no apologies for his continuing involvement: "As a member of the sanctuary community, and one of the growing number of Americans who are repulsed by the war we are waging in El Salvador, I am proud to be able to live my life in a way that allows my own alleged illegal actions to illuminate our nation's shameful policies. Let no one claim, as did many Germans under Hitler, 'We didn't know.' "

In Arizona, Cruz had all but completed his undercover work, but he still kept showing up at sanctuary functions. On Sunday, January 13, 1985, Cruz attended a potluck dinner at the Central United Presbyterian Church in Phoenix. There, some sanctuary volunteers talked about their worries that the government crackdown might be upon them.

The next day, they learned that they had been right. Federal agents began rounding up fifty-eight sanctuary refugees in Buffalo, New York City, Los Angeles, Philadelphia, Phoenix, Rochester, Tucson, and Seattle. At press conferences, federal prosecutors in Phoenix and INS officials in Washington announced that a federal grand jury in Arizona had returned a seventy-one-count indictment against sixteen members of the movement. Among them were Corbett, Fife, and Phillip Willis-Conger in Tucson; Mary K. Doan Espinoza and Father Tony Clark in Nogales, Arizona; and Father Quiñónes and María del Socorro Pardo de Aguilar on the Mexican side of the border.

That day, in an interview with the *Arizona* (Phoenix) *Republic*, Fife said that the real issue in the trial would be the legality of U.S. policy in Central America. "People will have to decide: Are they with a government that sends people back to their deaths, or with the church, which protects life."

Republic reporters also talked with Harold Ezell, western regional commissioner for the INS. "You break the law, you pay," Ezell told them. "And you cannot selectively enforce the law.

"America is a lifeboat," he added, "but it can only take in so many people."

11

Guatemala: "Apparently, There Is Democracy"

The deportees walked single file into an international lounge at the New Orleans airport. Except for an occasional joke among themselves, they were quiet. An INS officer in a pressed green uniform led the young men to a row of chairs on the far side of the room. There they sat facing the paying passengers as the Taca Airlines jet taxied up to the gate in the warm September sun. Within an hour, the men would be aboard a plane bound for Guatemala and El Salvador.

Three and a half years had passed since Southside Presbyterian Church in Tucson announced that the refugees from Central America were welcome inside its doors. By the autumn of 1985, more than two hundred churches, seminaries, and student groups had made their own declarations. National church councils and religious leaders had lent their support. The movement and the issue had been covered by almost every major network, newspaper, and magazine in the United States. So had the killings in Central America. According to the news reports, 1985 had not been as bloody as 1980 or 1981 in Guatemala and El Salvador, but accounts of torture and murder continued to inch their way into the headlines.

In Guatemala, the days when three hundred civilians a month were being murdered had ended. Now, the average was said to be closer to fifty, although, as always, accurate numbers were hard to come by. In July 1985, the *New York Times* reported that the Guatemalan Army was suspected of having killed at least sixty peasants in and around the village of Patzún after leftist guerrillas conducted a recruiting campaign in the area. Archbishop Próspero Penados del Barrio, who had been sent a blood-soaked handkerchief a few months earlier, said he did not know how to stop the killings. Gen. Oscar Mejía Victores, the Guatemalan "chief of state", held a news conference to deny that his army had ever committed a single human rights violation.

The civil war in neighboring El Salvador was at a stalemate, although the country was by no means at peace. Nearly sixty thousand people had been killed there since 1979. After his election in 1984, centrist Pres. José Napoleón Duarte had succeeded in reducing the number of civilian deaths substantially, but human rights workers continued to take statements about disappeared persons. Foreign reporters were also investigating reports that the Salvadoran Air Force was bombing civilian areas in zones controlled by the guerrillas. No longer strong enough to fight full-scale battles, the rebels themselves had begun to rely on terrorism. In June, four U.S. Marines were murdered when guerrillas opened fire on a popular cafe in San Salvador. In the countryside, they were kidnapping—and in a few cases murdering—village mayors. In early September, Duarte's own daughter was kidnapped.

In Washington, the Reagan administration maintained an upbeat tone in its human rights reports to Congress. Conditions in Guatemala and El Salvador were improving, they said. That being the case, they saw no need to change their policy toward the refugees in this country. During the previous fiscal year, 2,762 Salvadorans had applied for asylum. Only 117 cases had been approved. There were nearly 400 applications from Guatemalans. Only 5 were granted asylum. If anything, the administration was making the road to asylum even more difficult. Attorney General Edwin Meese was considering new guidelines that would force asylum applicants to prove that they had actually been threatened with persecution; fear of it would not be enough. Although a court backlog and an increase in appeals had delayed many deportations, Guatemalans and Salvadorans were still being shipped south.

Some refugees, such as the Guatemalan farmer I met at Casa Oscar Romero earlier that summer, were open about the fact that they had come to the United States to find work. Looking at a map spread on a picnic table outside the shelter, the farmer pointed to his village in Guatemala's Western Highlands. Yes, he had left to find work, he admitted. The army had burned his fields.

I had been listening to such stories for nearly four years in churches, living rooms, and refugee shelters. Some of the people wept as they told them. Others spoke with no emotion, as though it were merely the path fate had chosen for them. As a North American going about my peaceful, if sometimes harried, life in Dallas, Texas, I found the stories harder and harder to hear and forget. As a reporter, I also found myself drawn to the violent lands about which I had heard so much but seen nothing. In September 1985, I boarded a plane for Guatemala.

The country was now in the hands of Gen. Oscar Mejía Victores, who, in the Guatemalan tradition, had seized power in a 1983 military coup. Under pressure from the United States, which was increasing aid to his country, Mejía had agreed to turn the government over to a civilian president following a November election. If the transfer of power actually occurred, it would be the first time since 1970 that a civilian had governed Guatemala.

The new president would take over a country sick with trouble. Although weaker than a few years earlier, the leftist guerrillas had renewed their attacks in the countryside. Union and student leaders were disappearing from the streets of the cities, presumably the victims of right-wing terror. Some of the kidnappings had nothing to do with politics. Gangs of thugs also snatched wealthy Guatemalans and held them for huge ransoms. The kidnapping-for-hire schemes were but one symptom of a failing economy where the inflation rate was approaching 60 percent and more than 40 percent of the work force was either without jobs or underemployed.

A week before my arrival, Mejía had hiked bus fares from 10 to 15 cents and announced increases in the prices of basic foods such as rice, beans, and cooking oil. That sent thousands of students, workers, and housewives into the streets, stoning store fronts and setting fire to vehicles. By the time troops had quelled the violence, two people were dead and five hundred more were in prison. Armored vehicles had smashed down the gates of the University of San Carlos and occupied the campus. Once again, there were rumors of another coup. Perhaps the generals were not yet willing to let their power slip away.

It was raining hard when my plane pulled up to the gate in Guatemala City. A friendly security guard in a crisp blue uniform directed me toward the customs gate. In the confusion, I lost sight of the deportees for a few moments. Then I saw them being taken away by three men in civilian clothes. Each had a pistol tucked into his belt. As I waited to clear customs, the deportees were led single file through the crowd at the customs gate, then down a wide but empty hallway. There was no joking among them. During their first few minutes back home, most walked with their heads bowed.

"All is tranquil tonight," the cab driver said as we raced toward the center of Guatemala City. Except for pairs of patrolling soldiers, the rain-slick streets were deserted. The driver spoke English well, but he was not anxious to answer questions from a stranger. The riots were over, he said simply. The city would be quiet tonight.

Nearer the center of town, people were walking the streets and having late dinners in the small restaurants along the main avenues. The broken glass from the previous week's demonstrations had been cleared, but there were still signs of unrest. My hotel, the Pan American, was just a block from Sexta Avenida, the city's commercial center. It had been advertised as a place rich in Guatemalan hospitality and charm. When I arrived just before 9 P.M., the hotel's doors were already bolted shut. Rain-swollen sheets of plywood had been nailed over the first floor windows of the huge stone hotel.

The big trucks began backfiring before dawn. By eight, the sun shone through the haze of gray exhaust that rose from the cars, buses, and motorcycles that inched along Sexta Avenida. The sidewalks were lined with vendors selling everything from t-shirts and belts to cigarettes and shampoo from little wooden stands. Businessmen, clerks, and secretaries hustled past them on their way to work. Peasants carrying huge bundles on their backs inched their way through the crowds. Barefoot boys with battered shoeshine kits stood in the doorways.

So did young men waiting to change American dollars for quetzales, the Guatemalan currency. Officially, the exchange rate was still one to one, but on the black market, an American dollar bought three or four quetzales, sometimes more. In Guatemala's inflation-racked economy, the value of the dollar was rising by the hour. The government was said to be buying dollars on the black market to pay the country's oil bills.

The signs of Guatemala's great northern neighbor were everywhere along the avenue. In a country where most people make less than $2,000 a year, huge electric signs advertising Wrangler jeans, Sassoon cosmetics, and the products of dozens of other companies hung between the buildings. Kodak cameras and General Electric radios were displayed in the windows. The Cine Capital was showing *Rambo II, la Misión.* The poster pictured Sylvester Stallone with a huge machine gun that was only slightly more ominous than the weapons carried by the blue-uniformed police who roamed the sidewalks. The front-page headlines in *El Gráfico,* a large newspaper owned by conservative presidential candidate Jorge Carpio, said that the government would announce salary increases for government workers that morning. The raises would satisfy all sectors, according to a government official. In other news, General Mejía Victores was also warning that a demonstration planned for that afternoon by unions and student groups was not authorized. The security forces would be watching for anyone disturbing the peace. Another story on the same page told of a prominent union official and former Guatemalan congressman who had disappeared after being kidnapped off the street by "unknown persons." The city's firemen had not determined the identity of a mutilated body found the night before.

A few blocks away, the security forces seemed poised for more violence. Police with machine guns strolled among the vendors on the sidewalks around the central park that spread out before the National Palace, a foreboding, gray block structure built during the Ubico dictatorship. In the streets around the palace, soldiers in camouflage uniforms cradled carbines beside Jeeps mounted with machine guns. It would not be a good day to demonstrate.

I returned to the Pan Am at nine to meet Rebecca, an American woman who had agreed to act as my guide in Guatemala. She had been in the country for five years, investigating human rights violations and helping foreign reporters. Since most of the action had been in El Salvador, few Western news organizations maintained bureaus in Guatemala. Visiting journalists often relied on Rebecca for help. She had been recommended to me by a journalist friend who had covered Guatemala for a time. During several terse phone calls to Guatemala, she had agreed to take me to Nebaj, a small village in the Western Highlands. The army had leveled the Indian settlement that once stood there and replaced it with a so-called model village, where the army maintained virtually complete control.

Rebecca was having breakfast in the hotel restaurant with an American missionary who worked in the area around Lake Atitlán, about fifty miles west of the capital. She had come to rest in the capital for a few days. Rebecca said our trip to Nebaj would be impossible. The petroleum workers had called a strike. It would be difficult to buy gas in remote areas such as Nebaj. Beyond that, she had to stay in the capital to see what would happen at the demonstration. A few union leaders had been on television that morning pleading with their followers not to participate. There were also rumors of a coup.

By afternoon, the unions and the student groups had called off their demonstration altogether, but Rebecca returned to the hotel to say that the Mutual Support Group (GAM) still planned to march to the National Palace. GAM, organized in 1984, was the only functioning human rights group inside Guatemala. Patterned after similar organizations in Argentina and El Salvador, GAM was made up of the families of disappeared persons. Through marches, petition drives, and press conferences, they had tried to pressure the government to release their loved ones or at least to reveal where they were being held. Instead, government agents harassed GAM members and, during meetings with

GAM leaders, General Mejía himself accused them of being subversives. When this did not dissuade the group, its enemies turned to murder.

On March 30, 1985, GAM met at the Guatemala City offices of the International Peace Brigades, a group of Europeans, Canadians, and Americans who had begun living with GAM leaders in hopes that their presence would provide some protection. Among those attending the meeting was thirty-four-year-old Héctor Gómez, a baker whose brother had disappeared in 1983. Gómez, who sometimes led the chants during GAM marches, was among the organization's more visible members. A week earlier, armed security agents had come to his home in Amatitlán looking for him.

After the meeting Gómez told the others he planned to stop and pick up some dinner for his family and then catch a bus back to Amatitlán. Hours later, the Gómez family called other GAM leaders to say that Héctor had not returned home from the capital. The next day, firemen found his burnt and bullet-ridden body beside a road outside Amatitlán. Gómez's assailants had also cut out his tongue.

At the funeral, another GAM leader named Rosario Godoy de Cuevas told mourners that Héctor Gómez's murder would not be forgotten. On the morning of April 4, Godoy, her two-year-old son, and her twenty-one-year-old brother went shopping. The following day, members of the family were called to the local morgue to identify their bodies. Government spokesmen said the trio had died after their car plunged into a ravine. Western diplomats who investigated the deaths were unconvinced. Friends who attended the funeral wondered how a traffic accident could have resulted in the baby's losing its fingernails.

Through the summer, there had been so many threats against GAM that many of its leaders had fled their homes. Among them was Nineth Montenegro de García, a twenty-seven-year-old schoolteacher who had helped found GAM after her husband, Edgar, was kidnapped from a downtown street corner. She continued denouncing the military leaders in the press, meeting with foreign reporters and leading GAM's weekly marches on the National Palace.

The small, dark-haired woman was organizing the procession when I returned to the central plaza that afternoon. As rain clouds rolled in overhead, about fifty people stood on the steps of the Metropolitan Cathedral waiting for the march to begin. Most were Indians dressed in sweat-stained straw hats and handwoven clothes. The soldiers who had guarded the plaza earlier in the morning had been replaced by a handful of men in suits who stood across the street from the cathedral. Some of them had not bothered to hide the weapons that they wore under their jackets.

Carrying a long, hand-lettered banner listing the names of more than 750 missing relatives, the marchers began moving toward the National Palace shortly after 3 o'clock. Nineth Montenegro de García led their chants with a bullhorn.

"You took them away alive," she shouted into the bullhorn.

"We want them back alive," the marchers replied.

As they spread out before the palace steps, men with rifles watched from the balconies of the mammoth gray building. In the shadows of the entry stood three soldiers in camouflage fatigues and dark berets. Black machine guns were slung from their shoulders. Nineth Montenegro de García aimed her bullhorn at them and began to scream for the return of the disappeared ones. As her voice bounced off the palace's stone walls, the soldiers in the doorway laughed.

In the morning, there were still long lines at the Guatemala City service stations. Rebecca decided that, rather than risk being stranded in Nebaj for a few days, we would stay closer to the main highways. Just after eight, we departed the capital and headed westward toward the Mexican border, the same direction taken by thousands of Guatemalans who had fled the country.

The highway wound through deep, green valleys and steep volcanic mountains that jutted up into the milk-white clouds. Old buses chugged through the fog, their seats filled with passengers, their roofs laden with a motley collection of baskets, blankets, and produce going to market. Beside the roads, *campesinos* were walking to their fields carrying machetes and hoes. In a few places, young boys stood on the berm trying to sell parrots.

Every rock, telephone pole, and shack with a vertical wall was painted with the slogans of the various political parties. But despite the trappings of a campaign, there were signs that it would require more than an election to bring democracy to Guatemala. Army watchtowers and guard posts had been built at many strategic intersections and lookout points. In the villages where troops had not been stationed, members of the militia, known as the Civil Patrols, watched traffic from the hillsides. Just east of Lake Atitlán, once a center of tourism, the traffic began to back up. We came through a fogbank to see a line of buses pulled over by the side of the road. The passengers stood silently beside the vehicles as soldiers frisked them and checked their identification papers. This too was part of the atmosphere of an election campaign in Guatemala.

At mid-afternoon, we stopped in a village a few miles from the Mexican border to have lunch with some missionary nuns Rebecca knew. As we ate meatloaf and boiled potatoes in their small stone dining room, the sisters talked about the upcoming elections.

"Everyone knows it's a farce," said Sister Patricia. "Everybody who has ever opened their mouth has been murdered or sequestered. The people know that. You don't have a climate for a free election."

Sitting across the table, Sister Teresa was slightly more optimistic, noting that the television stations and the newspapers seemed to have been freer to report than during the last campaign. "I have talked to some people who have real hope," she said. "The people would vote, she added, "but they are going to do it very cautiously."

From there, the conversation drifted into their memories of parishioners who had disappeared or been murdered over the past five years, and of Guatemalan friends who had left their homes and fled to Mexico or the United States. "A lot of the kids are going up for jobs," Teresa said. "I guess you could call them economic refugees, but if the situation weren't so bad down here, they could find work here. They wouldn't need to go up there."

"But an awful lot of people who are not on one side or the other get killed," Patricia added. "If somebody is fleeing persecution, they are not giving them asylum. I think it's lousy."

As we gathered our things to leave, the two nuns returned to what they had been talking about before we arrived. A young man from their parish had been receiving death threats. They planned to smuggle him to Oaxaca, Mexico, and on to Mexico City. They hoped he could make contacts there with members of the American sanctuary movement.

The sun was going down by the time we reached Quetzal-tenango, named for the quetzal, a brilliant green bird that is the nation's symbol. With a population of about 100,000 it is Guatemala's second largest city. Unlike the capital, Quetzal-tenango is a quiet place full of cobblestone streets, low-slung colonial buildings, and cool mountain air. When Spaniards under Don Pedro de Alvarado invaded from Mexico, they defeated the native Quiche Indians near present-day Quetzaltenango.

Rodrigo León, who was expecting us, was out when we arrived at his home. It was on a side street, protected by a high stone wall and a thick wooden door fitted with a small peephole. His wife led us into a living room filled with antique furniture, wooden masks, and shelves of delicate china. When she learned that I was a jour-nalist, Mrs. León asked me several times not to use her family's real name. Her husband, a wealthy businessman, had been re-ceiving death threats on the telephone. Some of the callers had also threatened their children.

"I told them to meet me in the street like men," her husband said defiantly when he joined us a few minutes later. The middle-aged executive was still wearing his business suit. He was a small, dark-skinned man who kept a lit cigarette between his fingers at all times.

With a glass of homemade wine in hand, Rodrigo León said he was supporting Christian Democrat Vinicio Cerezo in the presi-dential election, but quickly added that he did not have much faith in him or any other Guatemalan politician. "Our leaders are all thieves," he said. "Vinicio is the best of the bad alternatives, but even if he is elected, things won't necessarily change. Most of Guatemala is corrupt," he added. "You used to get things by earning them. Now, the one who robs the most is considered the best. We're all like dogs after a bone here. We'll take it from anybody."

The main problem for Quetzaltenango was not guerrillas but hunger, he said. Few employers were paying the official minimum wage, three quetzales (less than one U.S. dollar) a day. Despite the rampant inflation, the clerks at city hall were still making 90 quetzales (less than $30) a month. At that rate, it took nearly a day's pay to buy a pound of ground meat. "You see people in the city who are dressed well, but they have empty stomachs," León said. The result had been an increase in crime, especially kidnapping for ransom.

"I'm doing well," he said. "But what good does it do me if my daughter goes out on the street and they kidnap her? It's not the people or the neighbors who kill people," he added, speaking in a whisper. "It's the government. And they don't give any warning."

The next day, September 15, was Independence Day. As Indians from the surrounding villages sold blankets and baskets in Quetzaltenango's main square, cadets from the military academy goose-stepped through the streets.

On September 16, we stopped in a small village outside Solola, a dreary provincial capital near Atitlán. It was a sunny Sunday afternoon and some of the villagers were sitting outside their cramped cinder block and stucco homes. Most were women. In fact, aside from a few schoolboys kicking a soccer ball around a field beside the Catholic church, there were few men to be seen.

The people were not anxious to explain the situation to two strangers, one of whom was carrying a camera. A nun at the church was less reluctant, although like most of the people I met in Guatemala, she asked that I not use her real name.

In the late 1970s, the guerrillas had been active in the surrounding mountains, she explained. They had come into the villages, given speeches, and, with some success, recruited supporters. At the same time, the Catholic church was organizing Christian base communities within the villages. When the army came in looking for guerrilla sympathizers, it made no distinction between the two.

"It started in 1978 and went on through 1983 or so," said the nun, who had been told during those years that she too was marked for death. "We encountered bodies all of the time. The village was just a dumping ground. Many times, not a day went by that we did not find a body."

The army singled out anyone who appeared to be a leader of any standing in the villages. That was why there were so few men left in the village. Most had either been killed or fled. For a while, other families took in the widows and surviving children, but in some hamlets hit particularly hard, even that became impossible.

The situation had improved since then, she added. Now, at least, some people who disappear come back — terrified and sometimes tortured, but alive. Some people are afraid to have anything to do with survivors, however. They fear that the price of their freedom would be agreeing to become an informant for the military. But mostly, the nun said, no one talks about it. They do not trust the guerrillas, the army, or anyone else.

Before we left, she brought out a box of handmade placemats and napkins and asked if we might be interested in buying any. "The widows make them," she explained.

In a village on the other side of the lake, the priest said his church had not been hit so hard by the violence. Since 1980, only about fifty of his parishioners had disappeared or been murdered. There were still killings, but lately the pace had slowed a bit. In some recent cases, the priest had even succeeded in getting the local military commander to release a few prisoners.

As we walked down the main street, he pointed to a mountain that rose up on the south side of the village. The sun had not yet burnt away the fog that shrouded its upper half. Although the army had wiped out the guerrillas in some areas, they still roamed the mountains outside the village. Every few months, the army sent patrols after them. Sometimes, the people in the village could hear the shooting.

The guerrillas did not have as many supporters as they had once had in the village, the priest said. Although they had given great speeches during their appearances in the village, they offered no protection when the army came seeking revenge. Instead, they had burned down some coffee plantations in the area, leaving many peasants without jobs. The rebels had also murdered two village administrators who were very popular with the people.

Mostly, the people were afraid of all sides, the priest explained. The guerrillas killed. The military killed. Even the local police commander was rumored to be a killer. It was said that for 30 quetzales, he would murder anyone. The terror may have involved politics in the beginning, but now it was a way of settling debts and personal arguments, the clergyman explained.

Walking through town, I stopped to talk with some carpenters who were working on a new school. One young man in a straw cowboy hat said that he was earning about three quetzales a day.

"Can you get along on that?" I asked.

"There are no problems," he replied, looking over my shoulder at the two soldiers who had followed me onto the construction site.

Leaving the lake area the next day, we passed through the small town of San Lucas Tolimán. Just outside of town, the main road was blocked by a huge tree. An old man sitting in front of a small store directed us toward a side street going in the same direction. The fog began to roll in again as Rebecca steered the car back toward the main highway. Up ahead, I could see three figures stepping out of the woods. Two wore the camouflage fatigues of the Guatemalan Army. They were dragging a civilian. He looked at us briefly as we drove past. His blood-covered face looked as though it had been split down the middle.

"Shouldn't we stop?" I asked as Rebecca drove by.

"Never," she replied.

Back in Guatemala City, the papers were reporting another attack by "unknown persons." Once again, it had occurred on a city street. This time, the victim was a Canadian diplomat.

Unlike the Guatemalan labor leader who had disappeared a week earlier, he had managed to escape his assassins. The Canadians, who had granted political asylum to a number of Guatemalans fleeing the military government, were unpopular with the right-wing terrorists in Guatemala City. Perhaps because the Reagan administration was promising a major increase in military aid after the presidential elections, U.S. diplomats had fewer problems.

Although they were still nervous about the outcome of the presidential election, U.S. officials in Guatemala took the view that the country had changed under General Mejía. Kidnapping and murder were no longer part of government policy although, as one diplomat cautioned, that did not mean that all violators of the new policy were punished. "I think there is an awareness in the government that they have to clean up the human rights situation," he said. "These guys realize their image has suffered."

The diplomat bristled when asked about the disappearances I had been told about earlier in the week. That was old news, he said, adding that he knew of "only" eleven hundred over the previous two years. "The biggest single problem that Guatemala has with human rights is that when someone gets up and makes a critical statement, it gets credibility," he said. "The benefit of the doubt is always given to the critics."

On the way back to my hotel, I stopped to talk with a Western diplomat at another embassy. He was still meeting every day with frightened Guatemalans who wanted to flee the country. "It's not improving at all," he said. "Because people count twenty bodies one day and nineteen the next, is that an improvement? How can you say it is. The people who say it is improving, I hope they all go to hell."

Besides, he added, no one knew exactly how many people were being killed because it was too dangerous for diplomats, priests, or anyone else to investigate. The Mutual Support Group was an exception, but the diplomat did not think the military would allow it to operate forever. "I think one day they will kill them all," he said. "I think that very soon, they must leave."

Despite several requests, I had not been able to get the GAM leaders to agree to an interview. But one evening, as I was having dinner with an American professor at the hotel, Nineth Montenegro de García and another woman suddenly appeared at our table. Although she had come to talk with the professor, who was in Guatemala to observe the elections, the GAM leader agreed to an interview. In fact, she asked specifically that I use her name, since she wanted the world to know what had happened to her family.

Nineth and her husband, Edgar Fernando, had been married for five years. Their daughter, Alexandra, was now three. The child's father had been kidnapped at 10 A.M. on February 18, 1984. Men in police uniforms had taken him from a bus stop at the corner of Third Avenue and Seventh Street. Edgar had been a student at San Carlos University. He also worked at a glass plant that had been having labor troubles. Edgar, 28, was active in the union there. Many of its other leaders had already been killed by the time he was kidnapped.

When Edgar did not return home that night, Nineth called his mother and other relatives to see if he had stopped off to visit. No one had seen him. The next day, Nineth and her mother-in-law began picking through dead bodies in the city's morgues and hospitals. As they conducted their grisly search, they met other families doing the same. Within a few weeks, four of the families decided to form an organization to aid the families of the disappeared ones.

Nineth knew such work would make her a marked woman, but she had nowhere else to turn and she was not ready to give her husband up for dead. "I just loved my husband more than anything, that's what made me do it," she said, as tears began to roll down her cheeks. "I almost went crazy when he disappeared. Thinking about him in prison gave me courage to do this."

She had gotten word that someone had seen Edgar in prison the previous December, but after that, there had been nothing. The government claimed it was not holding him. Since then, the GAM work had gotten even more dangerous. After the murders of GAM members Héctor Gómez and Rosario Godoy de Cuevas, Nineth had gotten threats. "They called and said, 'You will be next if you keep saying these stupid things,' " she recalled.

Some friends have pleaded with Nineth to leave Guatemala, but she has refused. "This is our country," she said. "Our disappeared people are here. We are staying for them."

When I asked if she thought she would ever see her husband again, Nineth reached into her purse and handed me pictures of Edgar and her daughter, Alexandra. "It's hard to keep my hopes up because so many of the disappeared have died," she said. "But I don't want these things to happen to anybody else."

On my last night in Guatemala, four leaders of the Coca-Cola workers union came to visit me in my hotel room. It was the only safe place to meet, they said. For nearly three hours, they talked about their ten-year struggle to form a union at their plant. The story was punctuated with the names of friends who had been beaten, murdered, or simply disappeared.

As our interview was ending, there was the sound of footsteps outside my room. Three of the men jumped up and ran to the door. After listening for a few moments, they left the room to check the hall, the elevator, and the stairways.

"From what they say about the election, apparently in Guatemala there is a democracy," the one who remained said. "But what there really is, is fear."

I awoke that night to what I thought were more trucks backfiring in the streets. But this time, the blasts came in quick succession. Too fast, I thought, for a truck.

12

El Salvador: "No Bloody Dead People"

Somewhere on the sun-drenched courtyard of the sprawling Salvadoran prison, Tina Turner sang from a portable tape player. Backed by a chorus of children, their voices soft and distant as spirits, the North American rock goddess wailed about life beyond the Thunderdome: "We don't need another hero. We don't need to change the world."

The tinny music drifted over the families filing through the gate with net bags full of fruit, candy, and chickens; over the khaki-clad guards with their scowls, black boots, and submachine guns; over the little knots of prisoners milling around the edges of the immense yard of concrete and dust. As prisoners waited for their families on a Sunday afternoon, they had cigarettes to smoke and tiny amulets and crucifixes to sell.

Outside the walls of Mariona Prison, a steady stream of yellow taxis and dusty buses arrived from nearby San Salvador. Old men in fraying straw hats climbed out, aging women with silver hair and wrinkled brown faces, young girls in thin cotton dresses, restless children in T-shirts and jeans. Some stopped at the tiny food stands outside the gray cinder block walls. Others walked directly to the heavy iron gate where guards waited to search their handbags and gift boxes. Once past the machine guns, the visitors trudged quietly up the winding road leading to the cellblocks.

They had come to visit their fathers, sons, brothers, and lovers. Some were thieves, rapists, and murderers. Others were in the section reserved for political prisoners. They included guerrillas from the Farabundo Martí National Liberation Front (FMLN) along with men guilty of such "subversive" acts as organizing unions, educating peasants, and treating the wounds of the wrong casualties.

The Mariona prisoners usually don't have to worry too much about having their fingers broken or their testicles jabbed with an electric prod. By the time a man is brought to the big prison, he is finished with the more excruciating aspects of criminal investigation in El Salvador.

Then comes the long dull wait. Few prisoners — whether petty thieves or revolutionaries — know when they will be released. Of thirty-five hundred to four thousand people inside Salvadoran prisons on any given day, fewer than 15 percent are serving sentences. The rest are "awaiting trial." The laws of El Salvador limit the amount of time a man or woman can be held in prison without being given a trial, but confusion and corruption stretch and bloat such laws. Most of the men at Mariona do not know when they will be released.

Dr. Eduardo Fialos Espinoza lived with the other political prisoners in a small gray cellblock just to the right of the main entry to the prison yard. Through hunger strikes and protests, they had won the right to hold meetings and hang posters on their walls. "Born, we have the right to freedom," read one of the hand-lettered signs above the small schoolboy's desk where Dr. Espinoza sat.

He was a small, wiry man with curly hair and a sparse beard flecked with gray. His cheekbones were high and strong. He hunched over the desk top, speaking quietly. His intense, bright eyes glanced repeatedly toward the door. The hallway was full of visitors. One never knew.

It was late September. The doctor had no idea whether any judge had even leafed through his file since the police brought him to Mariona in April. "I only know what she tells me," he said, nodding toward the North American lawyer sitting beside him in the cell. She was not certain where the case stood either.

Before his capture, Espinoza worked in Chalatenango province, north of San Salvador. With other doctors, he had gone behind guerrilla lines to help civilians fleeing the war as well as those living in the midst of it. He treated guerrilla casualities. When wounded government troops came to him, Espinoza helped them, too. As a doctor, he did not think it was his place to question a bleeding man about his politics.

In the spring of 1985, Espinoza returned to San Salvador to see a dentist. Because he knew working in the zones in conflict made him suspect, he did not stay with his family. Instead, the doctor found a bed at the home of an old college friend who lived near the Central American University. On the night of April 12, 1985, he and his friend came home to find a dozen or so National Guardsmen in the street. They handcuffed Espinoza, his friend, and all the members of the friend's family. After a search of the house, the prisoners were taken to National Guard headquarters.

Espinoza was blindfolded and stripped down to his underwear. After a few days, they took even those. He spent the next seventeen days naked and in darkness. He said his interrogators told him they had been searching for him for a long time. Espinoza already knew. Because of his work, his brother had been picked up and tortured a year earlier. The interrogators accused the doctor of coming to San Salvador to collect weapons for the FMLN. He would be treated well if he would just give them the locations of the medical facilities where he worked and the names of doctors, paramedics, and nurses working in the war zones. Espinoza knew dozens of doctors and nurses who had been tortured or killed. He would not cooperate.

For fourteen days, they called him every four hours. He looked into the darkness of his blindfold and made his declarations about medical neutrality and the Geneva Convention. They responded with blows to his face, chest, and back. Patches of black and blue spread across his body. A rib was fractured. They kept hitting. Between visits, they forced him into a crouching position so that he could not sleep. His feet swelled.

Some days, they grew bored with simple beatings. Then they would slip a tire filled with feces over the doctor's head. Or they might hang him by handcuffs from a beam so that only his toes touched the floor, or string him up by his thumbs.

Several times he was told to prepare for his execution. The first time Espinoza felt a gun barrel against his neck. They held it there. He waited to die. They did not fire. One day they put him into a car and went for a drive. After several hours, the car stopped and he was forced out. When they took away his blindfold, Espinoza was facing five men in civilian clothes. They aimed their guns at him. He waited to die. Again, they did not fire.

He was offered a new identity, money, and a new life outside El Salvador. Still he would not give them the names they wanted. They threatened to torture his family in front of him. Psychologists interrogated him through the night. On the last day of his stay with the guard, he had hallucinations. Someone told him later that he threw himself onto a soldier then fainted. He was beaten one last time before being sent to Mariona.

Some Salvadoran doctors in the United States had organized a letter-writing campaign in Espinoza's behalf, but the doctor did not know if it would help. Of course, even if it did not, Dr. Espinoza was still very lucky. Had he been arrested four or five years earlier, he might never have made it to Mariona. Even by the U.S. Embassy's conservative count, the death squads were averaging more than five hundred murders per month in those days. The murder count had dropped to less than one-tenth that by the time Dr. Espinoza was taken off to hang by his thumbs for the first time.

By mid-1985, the civil war in El Salvador no longer commanded front-page attention in the United States. Stories about the five-year-old struggle between leftist guerrillas and the U.S.-backed government of Pres. José Napoleón Duarte inevitably included the word "stalemate" in their descriptions. Gone were the huge offensives, city square massacres, and roadsides littered with rotting bodies.

The rebels still controlled land in the east and north, but five years of fighting had sapped their strength and reduced them to blowing up power stations, kidnapping mayors, and making occasional terrorist attacks in the cities. That June, four U.S. Marines and two American businessmen had been among thirteen people killed in a guerrilla raid on a popular San Salvador cafe. Three months later, the rebels kidnapped Duarte's daughter from a university campus. The guerrillas once had boasted of defeating the Salvadoran army in the field. Now they talked of a war of attrition and forced young men to join their ranks.

Thanks in large part to U.S. aid, the Salvadoran military was a stronger, better-trained, and more aggressive fighting force than it had been when the war began in 1980. International human rights groups continued to report on human rights abuses by the military and the radical Right, but due primarily to pressure from the Reagan administration, the number of incidents was far below that of 1981 or 1982. People still disappeared, but the kidnappers were more selective. One fact had not changed: except for the handful of cases involving U.S. citizens, arrest and prosecution of the perpetrators was rare.

For the Salvadoran people, peace remained little more than a dream the politicians described in their speeches. In the countryside, the Salvadoran air force was bombing villages in the guerrilla-held zones. In the cities, the security forces continued to prowl the streets in their dark-windowed Jeeps. Although the "death squads" no longer operated with complete impunity, they still managed to spread terror, in one instance by publishing the names of their intended victims in a newspaper.

The war had displaced more than 10 percent of the nation's five million people. Many of their homes and fields had been destroyed. Some had fled to refugee camps in Honduras and Mexico. Others had continued on to the United States. Tens of thousands were living in squalid little refugee settlements in the cities. There they relied on churches, charities, and the government to provide them with food, clothing, and shelter. The war had also twisted the lives of Salvadorans outside the camps.

The fighting had led many international companies to pull their investments out of El Salvador. A fall in the international price of coffee, still the country's biggest export, had further weakened the economy, leaving El Salvador with rising prices, a falling currency, and an unemployment rate approaching 25 percent.

As Archbishop Arturo Rivera y Damas told his congregation at San Salvador's Metropolitan Cathedral one Sunday, "There is one sure fact. . . . The people are suffering more and more from hunger, insecurity, and death."

On a rainy September afternoon when Salvadoran security forces were combing the capital for the president's kidnapped daughter, cars and buses sped past the Basilica, a huge concrete church on a main thoroughfare in downtown San Salvador. From the outside, it seemed like a quiet and empty church at midweek.

To the left of the main entrance was another. An old man, bent and nearly blind, answered my knocks, took the visitation permits I had gotten from the archdiocese office and shut the door. He reappeared a few minutes later and motioned for me to follow. We walked down a hallway into a small receiving room with no ceiling.

For a moment, two giggling young boys caught my attention. No more than three, they were sitting on a pile of wet garbage, chewing old orange peels. Then the smells hit me. Urine, rotting food, cooking beans, wet concrete, and sweat. I looked up to see dozens of people sitting along the walls of a dank, dark courtyard. No larger than a high school cafeteria, most of it was covered by a roof made of corrugated steel. Rainwater poured down its edges, slickening the concrete floor. Except for the benches and a few tattered hammocks, there was no furniture. As I peered deeper into the smoke from the cookfires and the mist from the rain, I could see more and more faces looking back. The boys with the orange peels giggled and ran back into the crowd.

A small woman wearing a white bandanna scurried over to greet me. About thirty, Juana was one of the elected leaders in the Basilica refugee camp. Wiping her hands on a soiled white apron, she apologized for the document check. Security was a major problem, she said. In the past, government agents had tried to force their way in. Refugees had been arrested when they left the Basilica. The archdiocese no longer allowed people to come and go freely.

"In 1980, three or four families came here to escape the war," she said, leading the way into the courtyard. "There are about four hundred people here now. It was up to five hundred." More than three-quarters of them were children. Many were born in the camp. Some had never been beyond its walls.

For the four hundred, there were seven bathrooms. The church trucked in drinking water every day. When it rained, there was sometimes enough for bathing. In one corner cordoned off by a slat fence, a pair of old women used boards to stir the contents of two black cauldrons. Squash soup for lunch today, Juana explained. Usually the church provided plenty of rice, beans, vegetables, and tortillas. When the refugees were lucky, there was chicken or meat once a week, sometimes oranges.

A naked boy ran past, playing with a corncob tied to a length of twine. He slid across the floor and tossed the cob toward one of the rafters. The old men sitting along the wall stopped their conversation for a few moments to see if he hit his target. There were dozens of corncobs hanging from the rafters. This one fell to the floor. The boy ran off to join the children watching an old Pink Panther cartoon on a battered television bolted high on one wall.

Some of the people had hammocks, but many slept on the concrete floor. "It is almost impossible to walk at night," Juana said. Sleep was also sometimes impossible. Although the lights were turned out at 8:30, the children often cried deep into the night. Then there were the sounds of a hundred little conversations and the rustling of men and women who could no longer wait for privacy to make love. For the refugees of the Basilica, quiet was a rare thing.

Sitting on one of the benches and stroking her young daughter's hair, Estella Carmena said she did not mind the commotion. It was more peaceful here than at her home near the Guazapa Volcano, north of San Salvador. Before she left one month ago, the bombs were falling so often that the people were living in holes in the ground. Her husband and her older children stayed behind to tend the crops. She and the four youngest came to the Basilica after the shrapnel wound on her leg became infected.

"They came from above and they came on the ground," she said, describing the military sweeps through her village. The people retreated into the woods or into the holes they had dug. Most of their homes were destroyed, but somehow they survived. It is true, she said, some of the people did give food to the guerrillas when they passed through. They gave food to the government soldiers, too. All of these men had guns. What were they to do? "Our crime is that we were living and working on the war front," she said. "But we were working for our children."

Her daughter scampered off to play with the other children. Estella ran a hand through her hair. It was almost silver. There were
deep wrinkles in her nut-brown face. She looked much older than
forty-eight. Two of her children were killed in the attacks, she
said. Her cousin's family was wiped out when a bomb hit their
shelter. She began to weep. "After the bombs fall," she said,
"sometimes you don't find anything but their clothes."

The sun was beginning to set when I arrived at the Domus
María camp on a hillside a few miles outside San Salvador. Once
a religious retreat, it now housed more than six hundred refugees.
Unlike their brothers and sisters at the Basilica, the inhabitants
of Domus María could at least get out into the sun.

Heber, thirty-three, met me at the iron gate leading to the
camp. He wore a pink shirt and blue slacks that were torn at the
knee. His two front teeth had rotted away. "This was the chapel,"
he said, opening the door to a small stone building. "Now, one
hundred people live there." He led the way to the carpentry shop,
where the few able-bodied men living in the camp made rough
bunkbeds for the refugees, and then to an open-air kitchen where
women were frying pieces of yucca. "Yucca again today," he said.
"And bananas, in all their glory."

Heber's two young children were always hungry. Often, he
gave them his food. "Being a refugee, you don't have the money
to meet their needs," he explained, watching his mismatched
shoes as he walked through a group of children kicking a ball of
rags through the dust.

Heber, a farmer, also came from the land near Guazapa. His
family would still be there were it not for his wife, who is an in-
valid. She could not run into the woods to escape the bombs.
When they finally fled, he carried her most of the way to San Salvador on his back. He held their baby in his arms as they walked.

When asked about his farm, Heber stooped down and, in the
dust, drew a sketch of his farm. For several minutes he explained
how and where he planted the corn and beans, how much fertilizer he used, how much rain the crops required. The farm was

the main reason Heber did not take his family to Costa Rica, Mexico, or the United States. "One grows to love the land," he said. "He works it and longs to return to it."

"When do you think you will return?"

"Being here like this, you have time to think about a lot of things," he replied. "But those are questions that are impossible to answer."

He was silent for a few moments. "The fact is, I'm a refugee," he said, finally. "I know what this looks like to you. I don't like it very much."

Occupying a city block near downtown San Salvador, the U.S. Embassy was guarded by a small army. With shotguns and machine guns at the ready, Salvadoran men in sport shirts patrolled the streets and sidewalks around the building, which was draped in a yellow antirocket net that reached from roof to foundation. A thick concrete wall surrounded the compound. Salvadoran machine gun crews manned the turrets that faced the approaching streets.

The embassy and its personnel had been attacked eighteen times since 1979. Like other visiting journalists, I was given a three-page rundown of the incidents. They ranged from bursts of machine gun fire from passing cars to the murder of the four Marines. The embassy officials take no chances. My camera had to be checked in at the main gate. My credentials were examined in the lobby by a Marine guard working behind a wall of bulletproof glass.

"The guerrillas are engaged in terrorism," said an embassy official who insisted that I not use his name. "They are more desperate than they have ever been. The war is going much better for the government than it ever has."

The embassy official pointed with pride to the democratic election that resulted in a victory for Duarte. In his eyes, restoring the economy was now the biggest challenge facing El Salvador. Many of the richest businessmen had taken money out of the country when the war began. Foreign investment had also petered out, leaving the government with little means to diversify an economy traditionally based on agriculture. Only an end to the war would reverse the situation. That was probably five years or more in the future.

"In the summer of 1984, the guerrillas decided to break into small tactical movements," he said. "That's the logical thing for a guerrilla army to do once they decide they are not ready for the 'march into Saigon.' That makes it more difficult for the guerrillas to operate, but it also makes it more difficult for the government to go out and get them."

The bombings of civilian areas had been part of that effort to flush out the small guerrilla bands and deny them support. When the international press began printing accounts of the effects of such air attacks, President Duarte established a set of guidelines designed to protect civilians from bombings.

"We're pretty well satisfied that those have been observed," the embassy official said. "We try to look at all the reports. We haven't been able to verify a single case of indiscriminate bombing."

He brushed aside the reports I had heard from refugees from the Guazapa area. Many of the people there did support the guerrillas, he said. "It's one thing to say 'no indiscriminate bombing,' " he added, "but another thing for there to be civilians nearby when troops engage guerrillas, or when a bomb is dropped."

In the embassy's view, the guerrillas were to blame for most current human rights abuses in the country. They were kidnapping city officials, attacking restaurants, and blowing up public utilities. The government had tightened the reins on the abuses by the military and the police. "The leadership of the public security forces and the military will not tolerate it," he said.

The thick scrapbooks were spread across a long table in the small second-floor office. Every grisly page was the same: two pictures of ripped and blood-splattered corpses accompanied by a brief description of when and where the bodies had been found. Every week a photographer for the Nongovernmental Committee on Human Rights took more pictures of bodies in the morgue and on the street. Grieving relatives came to the office to leaf through the scrapbooks in hopes of determining what had happened to their missing relative.

"They can say that there is no reason to be afraid of the army or security forces," committee worker Juan López said of the U.S. Embassy official's comments. "They don't feel the repression in their own flesh. It is the Salvadoran people who feel the repression."

Sitting next to him was Aníbal Breón, a law student in charge of the committee's legal department. "The press, the U.S. Embassy, and the [Duarte] administration present a picture of a country that now respects human rights," he added. "What we see is that people come here each day to denounce the security forces."

The committee, one of three active human rights groups in El Salvador (the Catholic church and the government had their own), was not the only organization continuing to condemn abuses by the security forces. A June 1985 report by Amnesty International complained that, despite President Duarte's efforts to end the brutality, "allegations concerning human rights abuses, including extrajudicial execution of non-combatant civilians, individual death squad–style killings, 'disappearances', arbitrary detention and torture have continued . . . although such abuses appear to be taking place on a more selective basis."

The report, which detailed a number of specific instances, also said that "military and security forces personnel apparently remain immune from prosecution for human rights abuses, including murder."

Like the Amnesty International report, "The Continuing Terror," a September 1985 report by Americas Watch also condemned human rights violations by the Left. These included abductions, forced recruitment, and execution of persons associated with the Duarte government or right-wing organizations. But both reports said that, despite rebels' escalating use of terror against civilians, the Salvadoran security forces were still responsible for the majority of the abuses. "We note that neither side's abuses provide any justification for the abuses by the other side," the Americas Watch report stated. "In both cases, the victims are the people of El Salvador. Their suffering continues."

Nearly 55,000 Salvadorans had been killed during the war,

most of them civilians. According to Tutela Legal, the church's legal office, 196 people were "disappeared" during 1984. Another 63 met the same fate during the first six months of 1985. Although the disappearances, the torture, and the murders continued, most human rights monitors noted that the violence against civilians had taken a different turn in recent months. Instead of simply murdering arrestees, the security forces often took them into custody, tortured and threatened them, and then released them, offering many the opportunity to become informants.

One such person was María Ester Grande, forty-two. After losing a brother, two nephews, and a brother-in-law to the death squads, she had joined the Mothers of the Disappeared, Murdered, and Politically Incarcerated, whose small office is just down the hall from the Nongovernmental Committee on Human Rights.

Sitting among a group of women there, Mrs. Grande said six armed men in civilian clothes had come to her home in San Salvador earlier and forced her into their Jeep Cherokee. When she got in, Mrs. Grande saw her twenty-one-year-old son, a soldier stationed at the San Carlos garrison, in the back. He was naked and tied with ropes. As they drove off, the men pushed Mrs. Grande to the floor and covered her face with a notebook. Eventually, she was blindfolded.

At the headquarters of the Treasury Police, she was interrogated for hours about the mothers' group. Who was financing them? Why did they cause such trouble? Where did they get the food that they distributed to the families of the disappeared? During four days of interrogation, Mrs. Grande was never tortured physically, but just before her release, an officer came and told her there would now be a "trust" between them. In exchange for her release, she would serve as his informant within the mothers' group. If she did not, her son would be killed.

She has not gone to see the man since. After being beaten and tortured with electric shocks, her son was sent to prison. As far as Mrs. Grande knows, he has never been charged with any crime. "He is in Mariona only because I belong to the committee of mothers," she whispered, as one of the other women put an arm around her shoulders.

The steel gate leading to the businessman's office building was guarded by a man with an M-16 slung over his shoulder. Another armed guard was stationed in the lobby. The executive worked in a spacious upstairs office with clean white walls and a large wooden desk that would be at home in any executive suite in the United States. He was an urbane man with perfectly trimmed silver hair and a quick smile. As executive director of a large business association, he was one of the leading business spokesmen in San Salvador.

"The headlines have changed dramatically," he said in assessing the situation in his country. "As time goes on, people realize there is not a war going on." The only signs of struggle, he added, were the events staged by terrorists, and they were designed only to keep the foreign reporters interested.

Although admitting that the economy was still in a tailspin, he said that the country had changed dramatically since 1979, when a reform-minded military junta took control. They were "fascists," he complained, not because they ruled at a time when the security forces were murdering thousands of Salvadorans, but because they ruined the business climate with their talk of redistributing some of the nation's wealth to the poor.

"Those who plead for the poor don't have a damn idea of how to solve the problems," he said. "They complain around the world that the only solution is socialism. Really, the only way to destroy poverty is to create wealth." One of the keys to that would be attracting foreign investors back to the country. The businessman thought that would begin happening in the not-too-distant future. "You can spend one whole week in the United States and not read anything about El Salvador," he said with a broad smile.

The nun was waiting for me in a small cafe across the street from a movie theater. As members of a women's social club laughed through a meeting in the next room, she talked quietly about the priests, nuns, and catechists she had known who had been killed. People were still disappearing, the young sister said, but not as many. She looked around to make sure no one was near. The bodies of the dead no longer turn up in the fields or on the streets, she said.

I was not certain what she meant until a few minutes later. While giving her a ride to a church school across town, she suddenly turned to me and asked if I could tell her anything about the new "machines" from the United States.

"What machines?" I asked.

A friend of hers worked as a maid in the home of a general. There she had supposedly overheard some officers talking about machines that would grind up the bodies of the dead.

"That's impossible," I told her. She said no more. Possible or not, she believed it.

"I think you are going to like this," the major said in flawless English as he wheeled a big JVC color television across the floor of his spacious paneled office at Salvadoran army headquarters. As director of the Armed Forces Press Office (COPREFA), Maj. Carlos Armando Avilés Buitrago issues press passes to visiting journalists. He also controls access — at least officially — to the war zones.

The major, a former artillery officer, was a muscular, compact man with a backbone as straight as a flagpole. His black hair and moustache were trimmed and perfect. His loafers were polished to a high sheen. A skillful dry cleaner had been tending to his navy slacks and powder blue sport shirt.

The major sat among the plaques, family snapshots, and antique rifles on his walls and explained the Salvadoran army's new outlook. In the past, he admitted, the armed forces did have a bad "image." Government troops did not always respect the human rights of the people. Sometimes it seemed that only the guerrillas wanted to win the hearts and minds of the people. But that had changed, the major assured his visitor. In the field, the army now took an aggressive new stance against the guerrillas. And on the home front, the military had taken steps to assure the people that they were on the same side.

With that, he pushed a tape into his VCR. The sound of

an electric bass boomed from the speakers. The major leaned forward and turned up the volume in time to catch the first screams of the guitars and synthesizers. It was Glenn Frey, former guitarist for the Eagles, playing a hard-rocking number called "The Heat Is On." NBC had already used the song for its video-age cop drama, "Miami Vice." Now the Salvadoran army had adopted it as its theme song.

For the next three minutes an MTV of counterinsurgency danced across the screen. The scenes changed quickly. The young infantryman with a fearless Rambo look was suddenly replaced by another soldier dancing happily on a misty battlefield. A squad of commandos with yellow headbands stood in a clearing, rifles raised. Three machine gunners stood in a row, weapons waist high, aimed to the left. In unison, they fired and twisted to the right. The scene was repeated three times, all to a driving rock and roll beat.

The Salvadoran people are tired of hearing bad news about the army, the major explained as he rewound the tape. That is why this film is replayed at least once a week over the government's television network. "This is dynamic," Avilés said as he replayed the video. "You don't see any bloody dead people."

He was right. The film was full of smoke, bullets, and battle cries, but like an old cowboy movie, no one bled and no one died.

Death had also taken a holiday from the air force video, which the major played next. On the screen, a lone Salvadoran pilot walked across a dark tarmac to the opening strains of Richard Strauss' "Also Sprach Zarathustra"—better known as the theme for Stanley Kubrick's *2001: A Space Odyssey*. By the time his jet was airborne, the music had changed to disco. Fighter jets raced across the screen. A helicopter fired a pair of rockets into a thick stand of trees. Smoke and flame leapt up from an unseen target.

"Isn't that beautiful?" the major asked.

EPILOGUE

"None of Us Ever Had a Choice"

Thin as ever, Jack Elder sat on the steps of the stone church watching the winos and office workers who shared the sidewalks that crisscrossed the San Antonio city park across the street. He wore dusty khakis and a T-shirt with the faded image of Augusto Sandino, the 1920s Nicaraguan guerrilla, printed across the chest. The former schoolteacher's hair was grayer than it had been when he had started working with Central American refugees nearly five years earlier.

For Jack and Diane Elder, much had changed since the days when they first began taking a few refugees into their home on San Antonio's East Side. What began as a personal commitment had become part of something much larger. Instead of being a sidelight to their lives, refugee work had, in many ways, become its focus after they left San Antonio for San Benito and Casa Oscar Romero. They had never been able to forget the stories of the Central American families they met. Nor had they been willing to trust the refugees' fate to a government that seemed intent on deporting them. Other North Americans had had similar experiences. Most, however, had not been put on trial for their convictions.

In January 1985, a jury in Corpus Christi, Texas, acquitted Jack Elder of charges that he had given three Salvadorans a five-mile ride from Casa Oscar Romero to the Harlingen bus station. Elder had driven them there, but the jury did not believe that act had furthered the Salvadorans' entry into the United States.

The celebration was a short one. One month later, Elder and

Casa co-worker Stacey Merkt went before another jury in Houston. This time, they faced an eight-count indictment charging them with aiding two other Salvadorans. Elder was accused of helping them cross the border and then taking them to Casa Romero. Merkt was charged with driving them from the shelter to the McAllen, Texas, bus station. Merkt was already on probation. Six months earlier, she had been convicted of conspiring to smuggle three Salvadorans. In addition to having her probation revoked, she was looking at up to a fifteen-year prison sentence and a $10,000 fine in the second trial. Elder faced a maximum sentence of thirty years and up to a $28,000 fine.

The trial lasted two days. Testifying through a translator, one of the Salvadorans, José Andreas Méndez-Valle, said that he, María Caetana Rosales-Cruz, and three young cousins, two of them males, had left their home in La Unión, El Salvador, because they had seen much death and feared that his two teenaged relatives would soon be impressed into the army. He testified that the group crossed the Rio Grande on November 7, 1984, and was met on the other side by Jack Elder, who then drove them to the shelter. After staying there for two weeks, he testified, Merkt drove them to McAllen to catch a bus to Houston. María Caetana Rosales-Cruz corroborated Méndez-Valle's testimony, although she could not identify Elder and Merkt as the two Americans who had helped them.

Defense attorneys accused INS agents of coercing the two Salvadorans into cooperating by promising them safe passage to visit relatives in Washington, D.C., in return for their cooperation. Merkt's attorneys presented seven witnesses who testified that she was attending a wedding in New York at the time she was accused of transporting the Salvadorans. Nevertheless, the jury voted for conviction.

U.S. District Judge Filemón Vela, who had presided over Merkt's first case, revoked her probation and ordered her to spend a combined total of 269 days in prison. Merkt began serving her sentence in early 1987. The government later dropped its prosecution of the first case. Judge Vela offered Elder two years' probation on condition that he leave the Casa Oscar Romero shelter and stop speaking publicly about the sanctuary movement. When

Elder refused the conditions, the judge sentenced him to one year in prison. To stay out of jail while his case was appealed, Elder would still have to move out of the shelter and refrain from talking to reporters. Again, Elder said he could not abide by such restrictions.

At that point, Vela again adjusted Elder's sentence, ordering him to serve five months in a halfway house for parolees. "You're a good man," the judge told Elder at the sentencing. "I am a person who agrees with the sanctuary movement, but I'm going to reassure people that the integrity of the legal system will be preserved."

Within a few weeks, Diane Elder and her three boys had moved into a Harlingen home that had been used as a retreat by local priests. Jack checked in at a halfway house in San Antonio, where he did maintenance work during the day and passed his evenings in the company of criminals getting ready to return to society.

"I don't consider myself a martyr," Elder said as the rush-hour traffic inched by the San Antonio church. "I don't like the word 'hero,' either. When you think that Ronald Reagan and Eddie Murphy are the heroes of this generation, no thanks. What we need, in these days, are teachers.

"The essential difference in my case was that I wouldn't shut up," he added. "But there are so many people who have been quieted. Those of us who can speak out have a responsibility to do so."

The pretrial hearing in the Arizona sanctuary case began in May 1985. Presiding was U.S. District Judge Earl Carroll, sixty, a conservative Democrat appointed to the bench by Pres. Jimmy Carter. Like the federal judges who had heard sanctuary cases in Texas, Carroll was not inclined to allow the defendants to use his courtroom as a forum for broad religious or political issues. Early in the proceedings, he prohibited attorneys for the sanctuary workers from arguing that their clients had believed aiding the Central Americans was justified under both international law and the 1980 Refugee Act. He also refused to let the jury consider the defendants' religious convictions or conditions in El Salvador and

Guatemala. When Carroll began interviewing prospective jurors that October, he told them they were being asked to consider a simple case of smuggling.

By that time, three of the original sixteen defendants had pleaded guilty to misdemeanors. Charges against two others had been dropped. The case still involved some of the movement's best-known leaders: Jim Corbett, the Quaker rancher who had begun bringing refugees to Tucson four years earlier; the Rev. John Fife, whose Southside Presbyterian Church was one of the cradles of the movement; Sister Darlene Nigorski, who had helped coordinate the movement after her experiences as a missionary in Guatemala; and Philip Willis-Conger, the young church worker who had helped lead many refugees into sanctuary. They and the seven others faced prison terms of up to five years and fines of $2,000 to $10,000 for each of the charges against them.

The prosecution's case was built around the testimony of Jesús Cruz, the former smuggler whom the INS had paid to infiltrate the movement. Although Judge Carroll said the use of such informants to tape church services "sullied" the government's investigation, he nevertheless ruled that the tape recordings could be admitted as evidence. (Ironically, after Cruz was cross-examined by defense attorneys, it was the prosecution that decided not to use the tapes, arguing that they contained too much "irrelevant" material.)

Cruz spent weeks on the stand, detailing both his infiltration of the movement and the operations of the movement itself. He told the jury he had gained the sanctuary workers' trust by posing as a sympathetic soul who just wanted to help out. In addition, he had at times talked of God with them and brought small gifts to sanctuary workers in Mexico.

Cruz said he had witnessed various defendants advising Salvadorans and Guatemalans to claim they were Mexicans if questioned by U.S. authorities. Cruz stated he had seen sanctuary workers lead Central Americans to holes in the border fence near Nogales and give American school uniforms to refugee children as disguises. The grandfatherly informant also detailed conversations he had had with defendants during planning sessions.

Defense attorneys spent their time trying to discredit Cruz, who testified he had earned $18,000 for his work on the case. Cruz admitted to having transported illegal aliens from Arizona to Florida in 1978 and 1979, before becoming an INS informant. Defense attorneys also alleged he had transported aliens on his own while working on the sanctuary investigation.

Judge Carroll ordered the prosecution to make an effort to find some of the smuggled Salvadorans and Guatemalans to corroborate Cruz's testimony. He later became angry when a memo from an INS official in Buffalo, New York, was introduced in court. The memo mentioned that an INS agent from Phoenix would be in Buffalo to look for some of the smuggled Central Americans. "This apparently will be a somewhat pro forma visit and only for the purpose of satisfying the court," it said. As a result of such evidence, Carroll decided to limit the amount of Cruz's testimony that the jury could consider in reaching its verdict.

Despite the judge's ban on testimony about conditions in El Salvador, defense attorneys did manage to present some to the jury through their cross-examinations of refugees called to the stand by the prosecution. One Salvadoran woman testified that she and her husband had left El Salvador to save their lives. One witness said that, prior to their departure, her husband had been arrested and held in jail for twenty-three days. With the jury outside the room, her husband later described the tortures he had endured. Another man said he had indeed come to the United States for economic reasons. He could not find a job where he lived. The factories had been burned.

In the end, however, such testimony did not sway the jury. In a surprise move, the defense attorneys rested their case without calling any witnesses, telling the judge and the jury that the government had failed to prove the charges against the sanctuary workers. In their closing arguments, they attacked the credibility of Jesús Cruz, condemned the government's investigative methods, and emphasized their clients' religious and humanitarian motives. Prosecutor Donald Reno told the jury it was a case of smuggling, nothing more. Nineteen weeks after the trial had begun, the jury began to deliberate. Nine days later, they returned a verdict.

Three of the defendants — Jim Corbett, Mary Kay Espinoza, and Nena MacDonald — were acquitted. The eight others were found guilty of conspiracy and other charges for their work with the sanctuary movement. At the sentencing that July, the eight defended their actions. John Fife told the judge about a fifteen-year-old Salvadoran boy who had found his way to Southside Presbyterian after all his family had been killed. "The haunting thought that came to me was, if that was my boy, what would I want the church to do?" Fife said. "We had no choice. None of us ever had a choice. Our only choice was whether we wanted to sell our souls."

Carroll suspended the prison time of all eight and put them on probation for terms ranging from three to five years. The judge told them he was sure they had participated in the sanctuary work because of humanitarian reasons and their perception that the immigration laws had been applied unfairly. Nevertheless, he urged them to work within the legal system in the future.

At the same time the Justice Department was prosecuting sanctuary workers for aiding aliens from Guatemala and El Salvador, it was also drafting a new policy designed to make it easier for refugees from Communist countries such as Poland to gain political asylum in the United States. Throughout the sanctuary controversy, federal officials had repeatedly cited the Refugee Act of 1980 in justifying the small percentage of Salvadorans and Guatemalans granted asylum. That law states that aliens must prove that they, individually, have a well-founded fear of persecution in their home country. But as the *New York Times* reported in March 1986, under the proposed guidelines, asylum applicants fleeing "totalitarian" countries would be presumed to have such a fear. According to the *Times,* a confidential memo prepared for Attorney General Edwin Meese stated that Polish asylum applicants unwilling to return to Poland because of conditions there would be presumed to be refugees under the law.

Aliens from Eastern bloc countries were not the only ones to get a sympathetic ear from the Reagan administration. A few months later, as the administration prepared to resume shipments of military supplies to *contra* rebels waging war against the Sandinista government of Nicaragua, the INS district director in Miami announced that he would no longer deport undocumented Nicaraguans apprehended in his district.

For the Salvadorans and Guatemalans seeking refuge in the United States, the policies remained unchanged. Like the European Jews who had fled the Nazi holocaust, they got no welcome from Washington.

In January 1986, the first civilian-controlled government in more than a generation took power in Guatemala. After becoming president, Christian Democrat Vinicio Cerezo Arévalo, himself a target of death squad attacks in years past, called for an end to the violence that had plagued his country's modern history. He suggested that the nation's judicial system be strengthened in order to protect human rights. A few weeks after his inauguration, Cerezo disbanded the Technical Investigations Department, the most feared of Guatemala's police units and one accused of being responsible for hundreds of disappearances and political murders.

Despite the election of a civilian president, the balance of power was still tipped in favor of the Guatemalan military and its right-wing political and business allies. Apparently worried that too much reform might trigger yet another coup, Cerezo showed little interest in investigating the military for past human rights abuses. Just prior to leaving office, the military government of Gen. Oscar Humberto Mejía Victores had granted amnesty to all persons accused of political crimes during his tenure. Mejía warned the new government that prosecuting military officers for past abuses would be a mistake.

In the months following the military's departure from the National Palace, the local press continued to carry stories of abductions, beatings, and bodies found in plastic bags. In July 1986, an Amnesty International report listed eleven cases that it urged the Cerezo government to investigate. Although the democratic election had given Guatemalans hope for the future, clearly it had not erased the potential for the same brutality they had known in the past.

To the south, the civil war in neighboring El Salvador was in its seventh year. Pres. José Napoleón Duarte was struggling to hold together a crumbling economy, keep the weakened but still dangerous guerrillas at bay, and maintain control of his own military. As in Guatemala, the violence in tiny El Salvador continued, although not at the levels of a few years earlier.

A May 1986 report by Americas Watch, "Settling into Routine: Human Rights Abuses in Duarte's Second Year," said that nearly 2,000 Salvadorans had been the victims of political violence during the previous year. The leftist guerrillas were responsible for 173 of those deaths or disappearances, the New York–based human rights group said. It blamed the armed forces and the right-wing death squads for ten times that many. Although the numbers were far below those of 1981, when an estimated 13,000 Salvadorans were killed, the report noted that, in any other country, a similar number of political murders would be considered appalling.

For the Reagan administration, the lower numbers bolstered its position that the Salvadorans being deported from this country had no reason to be afraid of returning to their homeland. It maintained this position despite a November 1985 letter to all members of Congress from Archbishop Arturo Rivera y Damas of San Salvador. In it, the leader of El Salvador's Roman Catholics urged the U.S. Congress to support a bill introduced by Rep. Joseph Moakley of Massachusetts and Sen. Dennis DeConcini of Arizona that would halt the deportation of Salvadorans for two years while the federal government studied the human rights situation there.

"To return the persecuted to the source, the origin, the cause of his suffering is an act of injustice in the eyes of Christian love," the archbishop wrote.

Noting that he had visited the United States a few months earlier, the archbishop added that "it was with profound concern that I was able to confirm through numerous testimonies that the authorities and members of the government of the United States have closed their doors and their hearts against the suffering of my people unprotected in a foreign land. During this time of war that El Salvador is living, deportation is an act which is contrary to the law of our Father, who asks that we 'clothe the naked, feed the hungry, give refuge to the persecuted.' "

The DeConcini-Moakley Bill languished on Capitol Hill for nearly two years. The issue was raised again late in 1986, when Congress passed an overall revision of U.S. immigration law. Once again, it got nowhere.

Raúl sat on a hillside at the edge of a park in San Francisco's Mission District. A few yards away from the lanky young Salvadoran, more than five hundred refugees and sanctuary supporters were holding a rally under a cloudy autumn sky. Unlike many of the Central Americans in the crowd, Raúl no longer had to be concerned about the INS. He had been granted asylum. Still, he worried about his family and friends back home.

In 1979, his sister disappeared. Two weeks later, his brother, a union activist, was murdered. A year after that, armed men came to his school in San Salvador and took away three of his classmates. Their bodies were found beside a lake outside of town. A few days later, five more students disappeared. Their corpses were found at a dump. Raúl fled after being warned he was next. For several months, he had been telling his story throughout the Bay Area.

"It is very difficult to talk about the death of my brother and my friends," he said. "One feels the pain every time. But you feel some kind of accomplishment because those people who are dead cannot speak at all."

He was asked what the future held for him now that he had asylum.

"It is difficult to think about having a future," he said after a few moments of silence. "Our future is in El Salvador. It is where our families are. It is where our customs are. Our land is waiting for us. Our hopes to return are very distant, but for most of us, the future is not here in the United States."

CHAPTER NOTES

Chapter 1

In addition to interviews with Jim and Pat Corbett and Jim Dudley, this chapter is based in part on personal correspondence provided by Jim Corbett. Information about Corbett's early years is from an excellent profile by Linda Witt, published in the *Chicago Tribune Sunday Magazine* on May 5, 1985.

Chapter 2

Jim Corbett's letters provided insight into the early development of the sanctuary movement, as did interviews with him and other Tucson sanctuary workers. A December 1979 profile on John Fife by the *Tucson Citizen* was used to supplement my own interview. The particulars of the Ajo disaster were gleaned from the dispatches of John Crewdson of the *New York Times*. Gus Schultz and Eileen Purcell were both helpful in providing information on the development of sanctuary in the San Francisco area. Agent Thomas Martin's memo was among the evidence gathered before the trial of the Arizona sanctuary workers.

Chapter 3

Vicky Martínez is a pseudonym for a Salvadoran woman living in sanctuary in North Texas. Her real name was not used at her request. Friends and relatives were also interviewed for background on her family. Several books were instrumental in providing information about El Salvador. In addition to Alastair White's exhaustive 1973 work, *El Salvador,* I also referred extensively to *Revolution in El Salvador,* by Tommie Sue Montgomery, *Violent Neighbors,* by Tom Buckley, *El Salvador in Crisis,* by Philip L. Russell, and *Matanza,* by Thomas P. Anderson. Anderson's book provided the quotes from Maj. A. R. Harris about El Salvador in 1931. Penny Lernoux's 1980 book *Cry of the People* offered insight into the development of liberation theology.

Chapter 4

Rodrigo García is also a false name for a real person. Friends and family were also interviewed in compiling his story. The book *Bitter Fruit,* by Stephen Schlesinger and Stephen Kinzer, was a great aid in piecing together the history of Guatemala, as was *Guatemala in Rebellion,* edited by Jonathan L. Fried, Marvin E. Gettleman, Deborah T. Levenson, and Nancy Peckenham. Also helpful was *Inevitable Revolutions,* by Walter LaFeber.

Chapter 5

In addition to the dispatches of Juan Vásquez of the *Los Angeles Times* and Alan Riding of the *New York Times,* stories written by John Burnett of the *San Antonio Express–News* provided information about Central American refugees in Mexico. Also of great help was "Guatemalan Refugees in Mexico: 1980-1984," a September 1984 report by Americas Watch. In addition to pamphlets and releases from the Chicago Religious Task Force on Central America, Michael McConnell and David Chevrier provided information about the evolution of sanctuary in that city.

Chapter 6

INS commissioner Alan Nelson's comments are from a June 1983 telephone interview with the author. The Rev. Dick Sinner's comments are from a February 7, 1983, interview with reporter Larry Stammer of the *Los Angeles Times.* Elliot Abrams described his views on U.S. human rights policy to *New York Times* reporter

Bernard Weinraub in an interview published October 19, 1982. Two books were especially helpful on U.S. immigration issues: *Still the Golden Door: The Third World Comes to America,* by David M. Reimers; and *U.S. Immigration and Refugee Policy: Global and Domestic Issues,* edited by Mary M. Kritz. My thanks also to Jeffrey Cole of Austin, Texas, for allowing me to use his unpublished thesis, "The Development of American Refugee Policy: An Issues Overview."

Chapter 7

In addition to interviews with several sanctuary workers in the Rio Grande Valley of Texas, reports from the Associated Press, United Press International, Scott Lind of *The* (McAllen) *Monitor,* Carlyle Murphy of the *Washington Post,* and Rone Tempest of the *Los Angeles Times* were used in reconstructing the events surrounding the deaths of four Salvadoran youths in October 1982. Figures about the influx of Salvadorans into the McAllen area between 1978 and 1980 are from an Associated Press story published in the *Dallas Morning News* on March 8, 1981. "Eduardo" and "Raúl" are pseudonyms for Salvadorans interviewed at Casa Oscar Romero in June 1983.

Chapter 8

The journey described took place in July 1983, while the author was reporting for the *San Antonio Express-News.* The real participants in the trip were given fictitious names at their request.

Chapter 9

In addition to interviews with Jack and Diane Elder, the recollections of reporter Scott Lind of *The* (McAllen) *Monitor* and Mack Sisk of UPI were helpful in reconstructing the events surrounding Jack Elder's arrest. A March 12, 1985, profile about Elder written by Myra MacPherson of the *Washington Post* provided additional details about his early years. Reporter Dan Freedman's piece on Casa Oscar Romero in the March 18, 1984,

San Antonio Light was also helpful.

Information about Stacey Merkt came from several resources, among them, a June 1986 profile by the Associated Press. Also useful was a March 31, 1985, interview by Ed Asher of the *Brownsville Herald.* Her quote about going to work at Casa Oscar Romero is from a March 1985 interview in *Sojourners* magazine.

Chapter 10

The chapter is based on interviews with several sanctuary workers in Southern Arizona. Especially helpful was Philip Willis-Conger. Details of his arrest are taken from evidence gathered for his first trial. The information on the INS infiltration of the movement is based on depositions and documents gathered as evidence for the 1986 sanctuary trial in Tucson. "Informers in the Sanctuary Movement," a July 20-27, 1985, story for *The Nation* by Sandy Tolan and Carol Ann Bassett, provided many additional details about Jesús Cruz's background and work for the INS.

Chapter 11 and 12

These chapters were based on a trip to Central America in September 1985. Most of the names have been changed for the safety of those I interviewed. Sources cited for chapters 3 and 4 provided background.

Epilogue

U.S. District Judge Filemon Vela's comments upon the sentencing of Jack Elder are from a report by Associated Press writer David Sedeno. Reports by Associated Press reporter Arthur Rotstein were especially helpful in summing up the outcome of the Arizona sanctuary trial. The Rev. John Fife's comments at his sentencing are from a July 2, 1986, *New York Times* story by Peter Applebome.